Coping with
SHYNESS AND L

C000193461

Dr Judy Bury, the General Editor of this series, has worked in general practice and family planning for many years. She writes regularly on medical topics, and has a particular interest in self-help approaches to health care.

Other titles in the series include:
Coping with Caesarean and Other Difficult Births
Coping with Aging Parents
Coping with a Dying Relative
Coping with Sexual Relationships
Coping with Skin and Hair Problems
Coping with Periods
Coping with Your Handicapped Child
Coping with Abortion
Coping with Separation and Divorce
Coping with Rheumatoid Arthritis
Coping with Ear Problems
Coping with Disability
Coping with Life on Insulin

Coping with
SHYNESS AND LONELINESS

KATE EUNSON

MICHAEL HENDERSON

With a Foreword by
JIMMY SAVILE, OBE, KCSG, LL.D

Chambers

© Kate Eunson and Michael Henderson, 1987

Published by W & R Chambers Ltd Edinburgh

Illustrated by Clare Herroneau

British Library Cataloguing in Publication Data

Eunson, Kate
    Coping with shyness.
    1. Bashfulness
    I. Title   II. Henderson, Michael J.
    158'2   BF575.B3
    ISBN 0-550-20516-0

Set by Waddie & Co. Ltd., Edinburgh

Printed in England by Eyre & Spottiswoode Ltd, London and Margate

Contents

Kate Eunson and Michael Henderson are both Senior Clinical Psychologists, at the Royal Edinburgh Hospital and the Leeds General Infirmary respectively.

Acknowledgements

We would like to thank James and Annette for all their help, and Maureen Morison for her original inspiration. Special thanks go to Clare Herroneau for the illustrations.

Kate Eunson, Michael Henderson

Foreword

Many people are shy all their lives. Most can learn to cope, but anything that helps is welcome. Here's hoping that this book will enable a lot of people to 'get up and go'.

Shyness can open the door to many other problems so it is worth trying to control it to some degree. Loneliness can be the companion of shyness so now we have two problems instead of one.

Mind you, shy people are actually liked by many, including me!

Jimmy Savile OBE, KCSG, LL.D

1. Being Shy and Lonely

Many people are shy; others are lonely. Some people feel lonely and shy. In this first chapter we shall look at what it means to be shy or lonely and how these feelings can affect one another.

Being Shy

We have all felt shy at some time in our lives. If we are fortunate, our shyness has been limited to only a few social situations and, although we may have felt ill at ease and self-conscious, no lasting problems have resulted. For some people, however, the experience of being with other people is a major and continuous problem. They are acutely aware of being unsure of themselves and feel very uncomfortable in social situations, often worrying before and after whether they have said the right thing or behaved in the right way.

Shy people are not always quiet people. They can even be people who appear to be brimming with confidence, who talk loudly and who seldom seem to be at a loss for words. However, they may think that they do not cope well in social situations and may have doubts about whether or not they have made fools of themselves.

Sometimes shyness can be such a problem that contact with other people is avoided if at all possible. Even day-to-day contact with shopkeepers and neighbours is dreaded. One result of this lack of social contact is that it can lead to loneliness and feelings of depression which may become additional problems.

There are a number of different reasons why people feel uncomfortable in social situations. It may be that they have always had difficulty talking to other people and have never really learnt how to do this. As a result they may be unable to make friends. Or it may be that, although they know what they should say and do, they are too anxious and self-conscious to be able to put what they know into practice. There are many other reasons why people might be shy. These include moving to a new area, changing a job, the death of a loved one, or an illness or physical handicap which makes them feel uncomfortable about themselves. Whatever the reasons, being shy is not at all pleasant. Most people have a desire for social contact. There is very little we do that does not involve contact with other people. If you are shy, even simple things such as asking for information or ordering things in a shop or restaurant can be major problems.

Being shy is really only a problem when it starts to interfere with a person's quality of life. If being frightened or unsure of others means that you are unable to do the things that you would like to do, then you have a problem that requires some help. This book will provide some useful advice on how to overcome the problem of being shy.

It is important not to confuse being shy with being quiet. There is nothing wrong with being a quiet person as long as you are happy like that. However, being quiet *can* be a problem when the quietness is a sign that a person is anxious in social situations and feeling very uncomfortable and that being in such a social situation is an unpleasant experience.

It is not the aim of this book to teach you to become the "life and soul of the party". This book will give you some help and advice about how to change the way you behave socially, and how to feel more comfortable and at ease with yourself.

Loneliness

The word lonely can mean "uncomfortably conscious of being alone". It can mean not having as much access to friendship and human contact as you would like. Almost everyone at some time in their lives has felt lonely. Feeling "different" and having problems with forming relationships with other people go along with loneliness.

Being lonely means more than being on your own. Indeed some people choose to be on their own and are quite happy with their own company. Being on your own is only a problem when it is not by choice and what you really want is to have contact with other people. The ideal number of friends for any one person

varies considerably. Some people are happy with a few close friends whereas others can be completely lost without a whole crowd of people. However, contact with a lot of people does not mean a person will not be lonely; some people are lonely despite having an active social life.

Loneliness cannot be seen. You cannot tell that people are lonely just from the way they look. Often lonely people appear to be remarkably in control of their lives and sometimes even a little aloof. Even the person who is the life and soul of a social gathering can be lonely. They may feel different from other people and be unable to share their innermost thoughts with others which leaves them feeling left out. They have no one to confide in but, by contrast, they can joke on a more superficial level with others. By appearing to be extroverted they are attempting to cover up how they feel. Therefore, many people spend a large part of their lives feeling lonely with those around them being completely unaware of it.

People can become lonely because they are shy and their shyness makes it difficult to overcome the problem. Others may become lonely for many different reasons and, having become lonely, their lack of fulfilling social contact can cause them to develop social anxiety and shyness which further handicaps them.

How many people are lonely?

Most people who are lonely think that they are the only ones who feel the way they do but, in fact, there are many lonely people in Britain. It has been estimated that around a quarter of the population is lonely at any one time. This means that there are about ten million people in the country who are lonely. If you ask the question, "Have you *ever* been lonely", very few people answer "No". A study in 1979 found that 79% of people under 18 years of age said they felt lonely sometimes or often, as did around 65% of those aged between 18 and 44. Approximately twice as many women as men suffer from loneliness.

All around us there is evidence that the world is full of lonely people. Nearly every newspaper in the country runs some kind of

4

personal column where people who are lonely are advertising for similar people with a view to making friends. Throughout the country there are dating agencies which do very good business helping the lonely to get in touch with each other. There are also singles bars and clubs where lonely people can go.

Why?

Why, if there are so many different ways of meeting people and so many people who would like nothing better than to make a few friends, are there such a large number of lonely people? One answer to this is that by its very nature loneliness means that people find it hard to meet and get to know new people. Many people are ashamed of feeling lonely and they feel it is their own fault so they do not want to own up to being lonely for fear of appearing silly. It could be that our culture has an effect on us. It is often said that the British are very reserved and tend to keep themselves to themselves. It is common to find that people do not know many people who live in their street. It is often not considered acceptable just to "drop in" uninvited to see someone, unless you know them very well. Therefore if you do not formally invite someone to your home you will not have the opportunity to get to know them better.

Who is lonely?

People can be lonely at any age from childhood to retirement and old age. Children may be lonely as a result of frequent changes in where they live. This can prevent them from forming good, firm relationships with other children. It can also mean that they repeatedly feel new and left out. Children without brothers and sisters can also be lonely as they have less chance of contact with other children. These feelings of loneliness can frequently continue throughout adolescence and adult life. Children who have problems socially often never learn the necessary skills required to make friends.

Many teenagers go through periods of feeling very isolated and lonely. It is common to grow up thinking that nobody really understands you and that you are different from everyone else. As people grow out of childhood they tend to worry about who they really are. The search for an identity can sometimes lead to periods of hating oneself or a preoccupation with looks and appearance. There are also problems to do with the development of a sexual identity which can lead to feelings of awkwardness and embarrassment especially when in the company of the opposite sex. Many teenagers complain that everyone else has friends but that nobody likes them. This is usually not the case and it is likely that other people in their class at school feel the same way. The recent trend for increasing unemployment among school leavers may aggravate the problem of loneliness among young people. Without the social contact that work provides and the money to do many activities, an unemployed young person's life can quickly become one of increasing isolation and boredom.

Loneliness can also be experienced later in life. For example, a person may be made redundant or get divorced which suddenly deprives them of the social contact they are used to. Although people who are older and more experienced might seem to have less of a problem, this is rarely the case. Many of them will have had a long period of time when they have never had to think much about making friends or planning a social life.

Women generally suffer more from loneliness than do men. Men may have contact with others at work but for many married women with children to look after and a house to run there can be little opportunity for social contact. In many cases before a couple start a family the woman has had an active work and social life which has to take second place once the children are born.

People who have physical handicaps or chronic illnesses have a tendency to become lonely. Often they cannot get out and about as much as other people and cannot use the same facilities as others because of problems of access. This means they have even less chance of meeting people and making friends. Their relatives may also feel isolated and left out. There are many organisations that cater for specific groups of the population. These can be extremely good ways of meeting people and for many they are a great source of pleasure. Unfortunately many people do not know what organisations there are and therefore miss out on a great deal. By its very nature loneliness means that people who would be happy to provide support and friendship do not know who needs their help. A list of self-help organisations for specific groups of people is given at the end of the book.

Loneliness and society

Although there are many lonely people, we are constantly being shown images on the television of happy people with many friends. At certain times of the year such as Christmas there is a general feeling that it is a happy time, a time for socialising with friends and family. It is at times like these that lonely people can feel particularly bad. Many of the traditional ways of socialising, such as going to the pub for a drink, are not really designed for lonely people. Women in particular feel very uncomfortable about going into a bar where they know no one. In general the British are very reserved. It is not common for strangers on a bus or train to start a conversation. There is a tendency for people to "keep themselves to themselves".

Why are we afraid of being lonely?

The biggest problem with loneliness is not being alone, but how we feel about it. Some people tend to assume that spending time alone is a sign of failure. It is also considered to be wrong somehow to spend much time on your own. It is probably our upbringing that leads us to feel this way. When we are young we are often told that we should have friends, and great emphasis is placed on who are good and bad friends. Children who spend a lot of time on their own are considered odd and this can be seen as a problem by adults. Similarly adults who choose to keep themselves to themselves are also considered unsociable and possibly eccentric. It is felt by some that it is our fear of being alone and our inability to tolerate being on our own that makes loneliness such a problem. Learning to enjoy your own company and accepting that you cannot always have someone to talk to can be seen as the first step to overcoming the problem of

7

loneliness. By learning to feel more comfortable with being on your own you gradually regain some of your self confidence.

How Can this Book Help?

This book will help you overcome shyness and loneliness. The examples described in this book are based on people with problems, who have been helped by the suggestions and techniques written about in the following chapters.

Each chapter is designed to help you to understand and cope with different aspects of shyness and loneliness. We suggest you read the chapters that appear most relevant to your particular problem. For example, if you have difficulty standing up for yourself, read Chapter 5 on increasing self-confidence and Chapter 8 on assertion; if you would like to make friends but don't know how, Chapter 7 will give you some ideas. Chapter 10, on self help, is designed to encourage you to put into practice some of the new ideas you will learn on how to overcome these problems.

2. Body Language

We often form an impression of someone before we talk to them. At times we can be quite convinced that we would like someone even though we have only seen them and not spoken to them. For some reason they have seemed attractive to us and it can be difficult to say why.

The answer is likely to lie, at least in part, in body language. The way in which a person stands, moves, sits, uses their hands, smiles or even nods can tell us something about them. These movements or gestures are all expressions of body language and can convey personal qualities such as friendlinesss, interest in other people, confidence and other qualities such as shyness and anxiety.

Being shy can be an appealing quality. Many shy people are surprised to find this out. Shyness has often been described as a tendency to want to stay in the background in social situations, and this lack of pushiness and quiet manner when combined with a genuine interest in others is indeed very attractive to many people. However, it is probably fair to say that the important ingredient is the genuine interest in other people as this will be conveyed to those who are eager to have someone listen to them and who love nothing better than talking about themselves!

Social Anxiety

Being anxious in social situations can be a major problem for those of us who are shy. Donald, a civil servant in his mid-twenties, found social situations such as parties very anxiety-provoking. He would dread going to a party and in particular, worried that his hands would shake and that everyone would notice how anxious and lacking in self-confidence he was. He believed this would put people off talking to him and that he would always be miserable and lonely.

Donald's main problem was that he was concentrating on his anxiety rather than on how he might cope. If he only thought about how anxious he was, he became more anxious, and a vicious circle resulted.

The way around his problem was to focus on ways of coping and to assess how well he was managing in the situation and what he could do to improve his confidence.

Donald wanted to look confident and acceptable even though he felt anxious inside. In order to do this, he needed to learn about body language.

Eye Contact

If Donald stood in the background at a social gathering, looking at no one in particular and often with his head down, people would probably think he was unfriendly or disinterested in what was happening. They certainly would be unlikely to approach him. The main problem here is that by standing like that, Donald is not making eye contact with people and so no one is likely to feel they have any connection with him or even an interest in going up to him to speak. By keeping his head up and actually making eye to eye contact with someone, Donald would

immediately seem more open to conversation and would look as if he were interested in talking to people.

Looking at someone is essential if you wish to convey an interest in them. During a conversation, eye contact also suggests that you are sincere about what you are saying. Avoidance of eye contact not only suggests that you are unsure about what you are saying, but can also give the impression that you do not mean what you say. So even if you find it uncomfortable to look at someone directly in the eye, do try to glance at them when you are talking and listening to them, even if it is only a fleeting glance.

If you observe two people having a conversation, you will notice that the amount of eye contact varies depending on whether a person is listening or talking. In general, people look more constantly at the speaker when they are listening. The speaker, on the other hand, will look at the listener in frequent short glances. The speaker needs to know that the listener is interested in and understanding what he is saying. He gets this information by looking at the listener's facial expressions. The listener will nod, look interested as well as saying "mm" or "yes" to show that they are following the conversation, and all this exchange of information through non-verbal as well as verbal means helps the smooth running of a conversation.

Facial Expression

The expression on our faces is one of the most direct ways of communicating how we are feeling. The most easily recognised expression is a happy one – a smile. Smiling is also a clear indication that we are pleased to see someone and feel friendly towards them.

Kevin, a likeable and rather socially anxious engineer in his mid-twenties, complained that he found conversations difficult to keep going. It was not obvious where the problem lay until he was observed in conversation with another person. Kevin had no difficulty starting a conversation and picked up whatever the speaker said easily and so, in terms of what was being said, there was no problem. However, the person talking to him reported that he had felt uncomfortable during the conversation and had not been sure if Kevin was enjoying talking to him. The main reason for this was that Kevin was giving very little feedback to the person talking to him and had hardly ever smiled or nodded during the conversation. By learning to nod his head when he agreed and smiling when found himself amused by the conversation, Kevin changed the whole situation. Both Kevin and the person he was speaking with enjoyed the conversation much more and, interestingly, they both liked each other more than before. The occasional smile and nod made all the difference.

What is important in this example is that a smile, even if it is a faint one, or an occasional nod, gives the person you are speaking to a positive message and this in itself helps to make the conversation more enjoyable. Of course, you can also give someone a negative message by frowning, sighing, looking away or looking at the floor and this will have the effect of making the speaker hesitate, and the conversation is likely to end more quickly. So, the expression on our faces quite clearly indicates what our feelings about the conversation are, and also whether we like or dislike the person we are talking to.

Some expressions are quite difficult to identify precisely. For example, anger, frustration, sadness or even disgust can show on

people's faces by very similar expressions, and unless you know the person quite well you are in a position of having to guess as to what their feelings may be.

Of these expressions, sadness may be slightly more recognisable. Often this is expressed not only by a sad expression on someone's face, but also by the avoidance of eye contact and general slowness when moving around.

Body Movements

Just as someone who is sad may move around rather slowly and keep their head down to avoid eye contact, someone who is anxious may not be able to stand or sit still. Often shy people who are particularly anxious display their anxiety by this constant motion.

Donald reported that at parties he often just did not know what to do with his hands which he described as "having a life of their own". By this he meant that when he was anxious, he fidgeted,

13

often spilt his drink and would accidentally knock things over. To avoid this he sometimes folded his arms across his chest but found that he often felt awkward doing this and was sure other people thought it looked a bit odd. He wanted to look and feel more relaxed. After trying out several ways of standing, he decided that putting a hand in a trouser or jacket pocket felt best. This posture certainly looked more relaxed and was less stiff than folding his arms.

If you want to look more relaxed and confident there are some postures which suggest this more than others. Keeping your head up so that people can see your face and keeping your hands in a comfortable position rather than fidgeting around all the time looks more at ease. Often people will put a hand in a pocket or perhaps rest a hand on a shoulder bag. Fidgeting and biting your nails can be distracting for other people as well as a sign of anxiety so try to relax your hands and if this is very difficult, hold a glass or handkerchief instead. In Chapter 4 there are some examples of how you might go about learning to become more relaxed.

Touch and Distance

Most people are not conscious of how close they are standing beside others. We tend to adjust the distance between ourselves and others automatically until we feel comfortable, standing anything up to an arm's length away from people we like and know well. We are also likely to touch them when we greet them or when sharing a joke or giving them some sympathy.

If we do not like someone, or do not know them well, or if they are in a position of authority in relation to us, we would tend to stand an arm's length or more away from them. The occasions when we are likely to touch them are probably quite limited, such as a formal handshake on meeting and departing or perhaps when ushering them through a door, when we might lightly place a hand on their back to guide them through.

As we get to know people better, and become more friendly with them, our body language also changes. We feel at ease sitting very close to them. We may take up the same posture as

14

them without noticing, such as sitting cross-legged when they are. As we become more relaxed with them, so do our bodies.

One fairly common problem in this particular area is how to increase intimacy through touch when you are dating someone without being rebuffed or rejected.

Peter had been dating a girl for two weeks and was pleased at how he had been getting on with her. He was sure she liked him as she seemed keen to go on making further dates and had even telephoned him in between dates to chat. However, on none of these dates had he kissed her or even held her hand. She had not made any moves to do so either and Peter guessed she also felt a bit shy and awkward about this as well. He was not sure what to do. He decided to take up the following suggestion which involved following several steps.

First he would take her to see a film they both talked about going to see. He would put his arm on her shoulder to guide her to her seat and then help her take off her jacket. Then, at the interval he would put his hand on her arm and ask her if she wanted a drink or ice cream. Later, after the film he would help her put her jacket on and take her arm when they reached the street outside. If this went well and she showed no signs of backing away from him, he would put his arm around her shoulder when they reached the bus stop; he would then tell her how he had enjoyed the evening and kiss her.

By this step by step approach Peter managed the whole sequence and did kiss his girlfriend. He felt quite confident about his approach as he knew he would go no further if she showed any signs of being uncomfortable such as pulling away from him. If she had done this when he had put his arms round her shoulder, he would have moved slightly further away and taken her hand again. In fact, on the night he attempted to kiss her, she had not rebuffed him at all and had squeezed his hand when he took hers which had increased his confidence greatly.

Remember that only you need know you are shy or feeling awkward in social situations. If you concentrate on your body language and what you could do in the situation to cope more effectively, then you are more likely to appear more relaxed and confident.

Showing an interest in others by looking at them and smiling is likely to help you a great deal as they will respond to your signs of friendliness by being friendly towards you.

See for Yourself

Why not look around the next time you are out and see what you can tell about other people from their body language. What do their different facial expressions tell you about how they are feeling? If you see someone who you think looks relaxed and confident, try and work out what it is about them that gives you this impression. If you see someone who looks friendly compare them with someone who appears less friendly – what is the difference? By using the people around you it is possible to learn a great deal about body language.

3. Anxiety in Social Situations

What is Anxiety?

Anxiety is one of the most unpleasant emotional states that we can experience. It is often accompanied by distressing physical symptoms such as shaking, sweating, a dry mouth, churning stomach, tense muscles, a pounding heart and feelings of nausea and dizziness. These symptoms are generated by our bodies as a response to threat or danger. When we are in a dangerous situation or one which we believe might be dangerous, the hormone adrenaline is automatically released by the nervous system into our bloodstream. This hormone has the effect of increasing our heart rate which in turn allows more oxygen to be pumped around our bodies. More energy is then available for our muscles. This change is designed to help us run away from danger or to defend ourselves. Other bodily changes also take place, for example the blood supply to our stomach is reduced so that more blood can be distributed to our muscles. We experience nausea, a churning stomach and alternate flushing and cold sweats. All of these changes in our bodies make sense if we are in real danger in that they prepare our bodies to react quickly to the situation. However there is a problem if people experience anxiety when there is *no* actual danger. If this happens, they are left with their bodies full of extra adrenaline and no increased activity to use it up. As a result they remain very tense and shaky.

Social Anxiety

Anxiety in social situations is relatively common. Many people will have experienced mild to moderate symptoms of anxiety when they have had to speak in public, meet someone important to them for the first time or attend a job interview. Most people

can sympathise with these feelings as they may have experienced something similar themselves. This occasional anxiety is not a problem if it is only limited to a few situations and does not interfere with normal day to day activities.

With some people, however, the symptoms of anxiety experienced in social situations can be very marked and distressing. They can lead to the person being so afraid of a social situation that he avoids it if at all possible. Such people will usually have become so afraid of the situation and have built up such a terrible picture of it in their minds, that most other people would find this exaggerated and unrealistic. However to individuals suffering in this way, their fears appear realistic, and rational argument will not easily change their misconceptions. This degree of fear of social situations is called a *social phobia* and often requires expert help from a doctor or clinical psychologist.

Typical thoughts

People who are anxious in social situations report thoughts which actually increase their level of anxiety rather than decrease it. Examples of such thoughts are:

> I'm going to make a fool of myself.
> Everyone will think I'm really stupid.
> I won't be able to think of anything to say.
> I'll freeze up.
> If I open my mouth to speak my voice will go all funny.
> My heart is racing, I'm going to have a heart attack.
> I'm going crazy.
> I must look weird.
> I wish I could get away.
> Everyone is staring at me.
> I cannot control myself.
> I'm going to blush/tremble/be sick.

As you will notice, these thoughts relate to the fears that people might have in social situations. They perceive the situation as a threatening one and may be afraid of making fools of themselves in front of other people. Very often the thoughts centre on a wish to escape from the situation. The important point here is that these types of thoughts are not necessarily based on a realistic fear but on an unrealistic perception of danger. Socially anxious people may actually believe (at the times they have these thoughts) that everyone around them is watching them, ready to pounce on any sign of imperfection or weakness. To them it seems that everyone is out to expose their inadequacies and that they will be made to feel childish or foolish, and generally ridiculed and humiliated.

This is only one interpretation of what is actually going on. However if it were correct, it would not be surprising if the individual concerned experienced a rush of anxiety symptoms and felt very afraid. Unfortunately the more anxious people become in a social situation, the more they believe that something terrible is going to happen and the more likely they are to become even more anxious. So rather than appearing calm and at ease, their behaviour is affected. As anxiety increases, they begin to sweat, blush, stammer or experience other symptoms of anxiety. These symptoms may then interfere with a person's ability to perform adequately in the situation. Drinks get spilt, hands shake, and speech begins to deteriorate by becoming jumbled and confused. Later the person may not be able to remember what he has said in the situation because such high anxiety levels interrupt concentration and memory.

How social anxiety can develop

It is often difficult to explain why any one individual develops a social phobia or anxiety. It may start when someone is under stress at home or at work or it may be part of a long-standing difficulty in relating to other people confidently. As often as not, it is very hard to remember just how the problem started.

Carol's case illustrates how anxiety can develop in someone whose confidence in social situations is already lacking. At the age of thirty, Carol sought help for her anxiety in social situations. She had always been a little shy and introverted but as a teenager she had several good friends and no shortage of boyfriends. She was divorced and had been living on her own in a flat for three years. She worked as a nurse in a large hospital and was, by her own account, competent in her work and well liked by her workmates. However she was lonely and isolated outside the work situation. Her difficulties began shortly after she and her husband had separated. Mutual friends of Carol and her husband had stopped inviting her out and she thought that they had probably felt unwilling to show loyalty to either one of them, and so had opted out of being friendly altogether. However, her workmates had invited her out to the pub and to parties. She had been pleased to go along and had even enjoyed these occasions initially. She did not, however, return invitations to parties to her friends, nor did she ever invite anyone back home for a coffee or a meal. Her own flat was small and she felt rather awkward about entertaining people by herself. Several months after her separation, an attractive man had flirted with her at a party and asked her to go out with him. Carol had enjoyed the flirting but became acutely anxious when the man asked her out. She thought that he had better know her "story" and blurted out that she was recently separated from her husband and all about how their relationship had turned sour and how she had not been out with anyone since. The man had listened and had then asked whether he could get her another drink on his way to get himself one and had then disappeared from the party. Carol had felt extremely foolish and ashamed that she had told him so much.

After that incident she rarely went out. She began to be anxious about men approaching her at parties, thinking that she could not cope with another relationship. She also thought that she could not tell whether they were interested in her sexually or in her as a person. She worried too that both men and women would regard her as odd because she did not have a boyfriend. Bit by bit, her social life shrank and her fear of going out grew. Thoughts such as "Everyone knows I'm on my own", "They're all staring at me", "I'm sweating – everyone can see it" became more frequent. These thoughts fuelled her anxiety.

Carol's problem began gradually and built up over many months. Sometimes, anxiety can begin suddenly. Two examples come to mind.

Malcolm had his first epileptic seizure when he was sixteen. He had fallen to the ground and had been incontinent. When he realised what had happened to him, he avoided all types of social gatherings as he was very afraid of having another fit. This fear persisted even though his epilepsy was well controlled by medication.

Donna could also date the onset of her social anxiety to a traumatic incident. She had been feeling unwell but had gone to a party around Christmas time and had a few glasses of mulled wine. She had felt very sick and vomited in front of about thirty people. She had felt desperately ashamed and very ill and had to be taken home immediately. After this incident she became very anxious at social gatherings in case she felt unwell or vomited. Because of this fear she developed severe anxiety symptoms which she mistook for signs of being physically unwell. She began to have panic attacks which are very high levels of anxiety and began avoiding social gatherings. Her social anxiety had then developed into a phobia.

Many people however, do not know why they become anxious in social situations. Luckily, finding out why you get anxious is not essential to overcoming the problem. Rather, learning to relax in order to cope with the physical symptoms of anxiety can help, as well as questioning the frightening thoughts and beliefs you have in social situations and learning to re-evaluate them.

Common Fears in Social Situations

"I'll make a fool of myself"

All of us have had this thought at times. It is one of the most common fears in social situations. If you examine this fear a little closer you will realise that it is a fear of other people's reactions towards you. The idea behind the thought "I'll make a fool of myself" is that other people will regard you as foolish, stupid or

23

ridiculous. There are several ways of coping with this fear. Firstly, remember that by having this thought you are predicting that you will definitely make a fool of yourself. It is very likely that you are *not* good at making predictions and have chosen the worst possible outcome – that you will actually make a fool of yourself. What you think might happen and what actually does happen are almost always different.

Let us imagine that your worst fear comes true. Try to be precise about what is the worst thing that could happen if you did make a fool of yourself. Some people dread appearing nervous and flustered. Others dread not being able to think of something to say quickly. What exactly do you imagine might happen?

Once you have defined this more precisely ask yourself why that should be so awful. It is quite likely that you are imagining something dreadful is going to happen. For example, why is it such an awful event when people criticise you or regard you as stupid? Does this mean that you *are* totally stupid? Do you value other people's judgement of you more than your own? If so, you are definitely overvaluing other people's opinions. Remember that people do not have full knowledge of your strengths and weaknesses. Only you know them. Just because you might do something that some people regard as stupid, this does not make you stupid.

What would you think of someone who made a fool of themselves? Would you regard them as totally stupid? You might think that they had made a mistake or embarrassed themselves, but no one is perfect. If we never made mistakes of any sort, we would probably be incredibly dull and predictable. Indeed making the occasional social blunder can ease a social situation.

It is likely that you would be sympathetic to someone who had made a fool of himself rather than critical or dismissive of him. The chances are that you have a set of rules for your own behaviour (e.g. I must not make a fool of myself) and another set for other people which are much more forgiving and much less demanding. Therefore other people can do silly things, or make mistakes and you do not think less of them for it; however when it comes to yourself, you are harsh and severe. As you will see, this is inconsistent.

Fear of fear

This is another common fear amongst socially anxious people. It is also at the heart of a social phobia. If you get anxious in social situations and experience distressing and uncomfortable physical symptons such as palpitations, nausea and sweating you may associate these symptoms with the particular situation you were in at the time. As a result, you dread the idea of the return of the symptoms and as you have connected some particular situation with these symptoms, you start avoiding similar situations. At least, that is what you hope. The problem with this is that the longer you avoid the situation, the more you fear having to enter the situation and so the fear of anxiety and of the situation builds up. You become afraid of experiencing anxiety symptoms and this in itself can increase the chance of you having these very symptoms.

> I'm going to lose control.
> I'll pass out.
> I'm going to have a heart attack.

These are all typical thoughts that you may have in situations that make you anxious. These thoughts are automatic in that they just seem to come into your head without effort and seem entirely believable at the time when you are experiencing anxiety symptoms. The most important point about these thoughts is that they are not true. The facts are that it is unlikely that you would pass out or have a heart attack. The symptoms you experience are caused by anxiety and although unpleasant, are not life-threatening and do not indicate that you are having a heart attack. Research has shown that when people are anxious and think the bodily sensations experienced are serious, they then become *more* anxious. Losing control is another common fear and probably people vary in what they mean by it. When asked about this most people express a fear of going mad. Anxiety is not a sign of madness. It is a normal phenomenon which everyone can experience.

Learning to Cope Even if You Are Anxious

Anxiety can sometimes be useful. Actors and athletes often think that they perform better if they are slightly anxious before an event as it helps them to sharpen their efforts. Learning to accept that you may not be totally anxiety-free is one of the first steps in overcoming anxiety. This helps to stop it being such a frightening and uncontrollable experience. Accepting that you might become anxious in social situations is an active process. Often if people just let anxiety happen and do not fear it or fight against it, its intensity will gradually decrease.

Sally used to think to herself, "It's just anxiety. I know these feelings well and I'm not frightened of them anymore. If I just stay with these feelings, accept them, and get on with what I am doing, they will eventually go away. I *can* cope with this."

Another way of accepting anxiety is to admit that you are anxious. For example at an interview most people would expect you to be anxious and saying something like, "I am a little anxious, but I will try to answer your questions as well as I can."

Even if you are anxious, you can still try to behave as though you were not. By behaving normally you can often reduce your anxiety symptoms. So if you are anxious during a conversation try to carry on talking, ask a question and then listen carefully to the answer. Do not escape from whatever you are doing. Continue in the situation even if you may not be giving a perfect performance. Running away from the situation may make your anxiety decrease but the fear of returning to the same situation will increase. Stay there, keep doing what you have started and as your anxiety decreases your confidence will increase. If you do this make sure that you remind yourself that you have coped when it is over. The next time you are in the same situation you will be able to cope with it more readily.

Alcohol and tranquillisers

Alcohol is readily available at social functions and if you are anxious in these situations, it is very easy to drink too much too quickly. It is not advisable to drink alcohol as a way of reducing anxiety. The reason for this is that it can lead to excessive drinking and this itself can produce anxiety symptoms.

Anti-anxiety drugs can be very helpful. There is a wide variety of anti-anxiety drugs that can be prescribed by doctors. The most common of these are either tranquillisers such as benzadiazepines (Librium, Valium) or beta-receptor blocking drugs (propranalol).They are only helpful as short term aids and are not a long term solution to the problem of social anxiety. They should *only* be taken as directed by a doctor and it is not advisable to take tablets prescribed for someone else.

Relaxation methods

Learning to relax is a very effective way of gaining control over anxiety symptoms. It is a skill and, like any other skill, to learn it requires practice.

The following is a brief method of relaxing.

1. Sit in a comfortable chair. Make sure that the room is warm and quiet and that you will not be disturbed.

2. Concentrate on your breathing. Just breathe in and out freely and easily. Notice how you relax a little as you breathe out.

3. Now breathe in deeply. Hold it for a second and then breathe out slowly and steadily. Now breathe normally. Notice again how you relax as you breathe out. Repeat this a few times.

You can use this breathing technique to control your feelings of physical tension and anxiety. By controlling the amount of breath you take in and push out, you alter the physiological processes in your body and this decreases anxiety.

There is a longer method of relaxation involving tensing and relaxing your muscles which is explained fully in the next chapter, along with a number of other suggestions.

27

Summary

1. Anxiety in social situations is unrealistic. Your body is reacting to the situation *as if* you were in real danger. In reality there is no danger.

2. Your mind is also reacting to the situation as if you were in danger which is why you feel afraid and self-conscious. The thoughts you are having are *not* based on reality and only make you feel worse. Ask yourself three questions to challenge these thoughts:
   a) What is the evidence for what I am thinking?
   b) Is there an alternative way of looking at this situation?
   c) What might happen if my worst fear came true?

Concentrate on the facts before you, not on your fears.

3. Relaxation can help you gain control over the unpleasant physical symptoms of anxiety. The more you practise the more confident you will become in being able to cope with these symptoms in social situations.

4. Do not avoid situations that make you anxious. This only serves to make your fear of situations worse. Rather learn to cope in the situation by relaxing, challenging your anxiety-provoking thoughts and by behaving in as normal a manner as you can. By doing this, you will overcome your fears and your confidence will increase.

4. Relaxation

Many people find it difficult to relax; for anxious people this is often especially so in social situations. Feelings of tension can occur even when the person is not in the situation they find difficult. This is usually because they are thinking about the situation and how hard it will be.

Learning to relax is a useful skill that can help greatly in reducing the uncomfortable feelings of anxiety that we all experience at some time or another. This chapter will explain a number of ways that you can learn to relax. The secret of learning any skill is practice and relaxation is no exception. It is important to practise regularly the method you choose in order to gain maximum benefit.

Day to Day Relaxation

In addition to the specific exercises outlined in the next section, it is a good idea to do something relaxing every day. Try to set aside some time every day to relax and unwind, if possible this should be for around 30 minutes. If you live with other people you might need to train them to accept that you wish to be left alone at a certain time each day. For some people just arranging their day to have 30 minutes on their own makes a great difference to their lives.

If you are not used to relaxing you will need to experiment to see what you can do that has the best effect. Why not try some of these suggestions and see what effect they have on you. There may well be some other ideas you have that would suit you better. Try them and see what is best for you.

- have a long hot bath
- read an easy book
- listen to soft music (with headphones is better)

- lie on your bed and spend a million pounds in your head
- imagine you are lying on a hot beach in Spain
- draw a picture/doodle.

Some people find exercise relaxing, for example:

- going for a walk
- running on the spot for two minutes
- doing an exercise tape.

Specific Relaxation Exercises

In Chapter 3, on social anxiety, a simple breathing exercise is given. This is a quick way of coping with anxiety and tension, especially if you are out with other people. Another, longer, method which you need to practise at home is the skill of muscle relaxation. Once learnt and practised regularly it is possible to use part of these exercises in difficult situations without anyone knowing what you are doing. The exercises consist of tensing and relaxing the various muscle groups in the body. As you are learning this method you should become more able to tell if any part of your body is too tense. This means that you will be in a position to remedy this before you get very tense and uncomfortable. You should not expect to be able to relax completely when you first start doing these exercises. Gradual progress over a number of days is a more realistic aim. Some people find that they feel silly when they first start doing the exercises explained in the next section. However, they soon get used to it and find them helpful.

Muscle Relaxation Exercises

Do not hurry through the exercises; take your time. Master each section before moving on to the next. You will need at least 20 minutes each day to practise. Either lie on top of a bed or sit in a comfortable chair. Each section will take about five minutes. Ideally all four sections should be tried when you first start.

Section 1: Arms

Clench your right hand, notice how tense it becomes, hold it for a moment, and then let it relax.
Now let your hand become as loose and relaxed as possible.
Do this a second time.

Repeat this with your left hand.

Do this with both hands together.

Each time notice the difference between tension and relaxation.
Bend your arms at the elbows and tense your muscles.
Now let your arms return to a comfortable position and relax.
Repeat this once.

Stretch your arms out in front of you and tense them in this way.
Now let your arms return to a comfortable position and relax.
Repeat this once.

Now stay still and see if you can let a relaxed feeling spread to the rest of your body.

Section 2: Face, neck and shoulders

Make yourself as comfortable as possible and let your muscles go loose and heavy.

Screw up your face; clench your jaw, frown, close your eyes tightly and purse your lips together.
Notice how tense your face is.

Next, let go of tension in your face and imagine your skin being perfectly smooth and the expression on your face one of calmness.
Repeat this once.

Bend your head forward, move it to one side, let it roll back slowly and then move it to the other side.
Now let your head return to a comfortable position and relax.
Repeat this once.

Shrug your shoulders up towards your ears and then push them forward and back.
Let them drop back to a comfortable position and relax.
Repeat this once.

31

Remember – each time you tense and then relax, notice the different feelings each produces.

Try to become more relaxed all over your body.

Section 3: Chest, stomach and back

Let all your muscles go loose and heavy.

Concentrate on your breathing, breathe slowly and smoothly in and out.

Notice how you relax a little each time you breathe out.

Do not breathe too deeply, just gently take smooth breaths.

Tighten your stomach muscles by pushing your stomach out. Now relax your stomach.

Tighten your stomach muscles by pulling your stomach in. Now relax your stomach.

Once again, tighten your stomach muscles by pushing out, hold the tension for a few seconds and then relax your stomach.

Tighten your stomach muscles by pulling your stomach in and then relax once more.

Each time you do this notice the difference in feeling between tension and relaxation.

Notice how good you feel when your stomach is more relaxed.

Arch your back very gently and feel the tension in your spine. Try to locate the tension in your lower back.

Now settle back comfortably and relax.

Arch your back again and then relax once more.

Lie still and try to let go of all the tension in your body and relax.

Try to notice if any feelings of tension have crept back into your arms, face or neck. If they have, concentrate on getting rid of this tension; you may need to tense and relax that particular part of your body again before you continue.

Section 4: Legs

Let all your muscles go loose and heavy.

Stretch your legs out in front of you as if you were trying to grow taller.

Hold this for a few seconds and then relax your legs.

Bend your feet up towards you, hold the tension for a moment and then relax them.

Now point your toes away from your face and tense them this way.
Once more notice the tension, hold it for a moment and then relax your feet.

Repeat these instructions once more.

Now lie comfortably and let all your muscles go loose and heavy.

Try and let the relaxed feeling spread over your body.
Feel how heavy and relaxed you have become.

Take in a couple of slow deep breaths, letting the air out slowly and notice how with each breath you feel more relaxed.

As you lie still, concentrate on the feelings of relaxation and calmness. Once again check that any tension has not crept back anywhere. If it has, relax the tense part of your body, and then continue enjoying the calm feeling.

Continue to lie in this comfortable way for a while.
When you feel ready to get up count slowly backwards from three to one and then get up SLOWLY! You will feel much more relaxed and refreshed.

Note

The aim of these exercises is to teach you to recognise when a part of your body is tense. Once you have mastered this you should be able to deal with the tension by doing only part of the exercises. Many people find that with practice they can manage to do some of the exercises while they are out with other people without anyone noticing. Even if you do not manage this, you could always go to the bathroom for five minutes and do one part such as the arm exercises to help you feel calmer and more in control of your own body.

33

Relaxation Using Imagery

Another relaxation technique is to use imagery. Imagery means creating pictures in your mind, in this case pleasant, calming pictures. Most people have their ideal scene which means complete calmness to them. This is often somewhere out of doors such as a quiet beach abroad or lying by a country stream. It is possible to use a pleasant image to relax using the method outlined below. This might sound odd but many people find this way of relaxing helpful. Why not give it a go and see if it helps you?

1. Find somewhere quiet to sit or lie.

2. Choose a pleasant scene to imagine.

3. Imagine you are there, with nothing to worry about and nothing to do.

4. Gradually build up the scene in your mind, the sights, sounds and smells you would experience if you were actually there.

5. If it is an image of somewhere hot such as a beach, imagine you are feeling so pleasantly warm that it would be too much of an effort to move a muscle.

You will need to practise this a few times before you manage to feel as if you really are there. If possible you could get a tape or record with sound effects that help you to build the scene in your mind. Your local library may well have sound effects records that you could borrow.

Summary

Everyone will gain some benefit from learning to relax. How you decide to relax is entirely up to you. There is no doubt that the best method for any person is the one that most suits them and their lifestyle. Experiment to find out the way that suits you best. The important things are to practise on a regular basis and to try and include relaxation as a part of your daily routine.

5. Increasing Self-Confidence

Lonely and shy people often do not like themselves and can be convinced that other people will not like them. The key problem here is that they are not necessarily less likeable than other people but they think or believe that they are. As a result they suffer from low self esteem and are plagued by self-critical thoughts such as "I'm not as good as other people", "No one likes me" or "I always make a fool of myself". The more they criticise and dislike themselves, the more they drive other people away, rather than attracting them. Unfortunately they rarely realise that the problem is not that other people do not like them but that they do not like themselves.

Learning to Like Yourself

Sometimes people who think that they are not likeable present themselves to others in a negative way. They can appear grumpy, easily irritated and often seem to be complaining about other people. It may be that not liking themselves makes them quick to spot unattractive aspects of other people. What comes across to others, however, is that they seem to be rather bitter, hostile and critical of others. As a result, people are driven away from, rather than attracted to them. Nobody particularly likes to spend time in the company of someone who moans, criticises and generally runs other people down. Unfortunately, many lonely and shy people do not realise that their negative image of themselves is reflected in the way they talk about others and behave towards them.

The solution to not liking yourself is not in making friends or having an intimate relationship with someone else. The answer is not in other people, but in learning to accept and like yourself. Rather than being your worst critic, try to become your own best

friend. It is unlikely that you would tolerate a friend who told you that you were boring, not interesting or stupid and yet this is possibly what you keep telling yourself. We all feel better about ourselves and prefer to be with people who are interested in us and who bring out the best in us. So try to stop repeatedly picking faults in yourself and begin to be more forgiving and kinder to yourself. Break the habit of always concentrating on your worst points and learn to evaluate yourself realistically. This is not positive thinking nor is it self-deception. Realistically you will have some assets and you are probably not making the most of them.

It might be a good idea to make a list of what your strengths and weaknesses are right now. If you find this rather difficult, imagine what someone who knows you well might say about you if they were asked. Here is an example.

Personal Balance Sheet

Strong Points	Weak Points
good listener	*don't like criticism*
kind	*sulky*
sense of humour	*irritable*
can amuse myself	*take my bad moods out on other people*
generous	
interested in others	
conscientious	

For the present, concentrate on your strengths. Are you making the most of them? For example, if you think that you are a good listener, do you often show this? Do you ask people about themselves and encourage them to talk so that you can demonstrate one of your strengths? It is quite likely that you have not acknowledged before that you have assets. Now that you have a list of them, make sure that you remind yourself of these qualities and try to show them off a little. If you have assets, "use them—don't lose them".

Getting Close to People

Most lonely and shy people long to have a close, loving relationship with someone. Paradoxically, they often seem to avoid getting close to people in case a relationship does develop. They also seem to run away as soon as anyone shows an interest in them. This is often because their lack of self-confidence leads them to think that any relationship they make will not work out and that it will be their fault. As a result, they avoid making the first moves in starting friendships and so never develop the confidence to pursue a friendship even on a casual level.

John, a twenty-two year old student, had always felt shy. He had been a quiet, studious child who had been teased a bit at school. Much of his loneliness was due to his fear of getting close to people as he thought they would reject him. A vicious circle resulted. He never attempted to make friends because he thought that people would not like him. Then as a result of having no friends, he concluded that this must be true.

When he had a conversation with a fellow student, he usually interpreted their reactions as meaning rejection. For example if someone smiled, he thought "They are just feeling sorry for me", if someone looked over his shoulder whilst talking to him, he thought "They're bored". When John realised the trap in his thinking he set up an experiment to see if he could change his negative thinking during conversations. He would deliberately concentrate on aspects of a conversation rather than whether someone liked him or not. He would ask himself if he was enjoying himself, or was finding the other person amusing, interesting or boring. This experiment was successful in that he found himself being interested in what other people were actually saying. He also made the important discovery that he was bored at times during conversations. At parties, when he talked to someone he knew and liked he became aware that he felt as though he was trapped. He would think "I've got to get away before I say too much. They wouldn't like me if they knew what I was really like". By deliberately telling himself that he could be in control of how much he told people about himself and that relationships develop at the pace set by both people, not just one person, he became more confident in these situations too.

After a series of such experiments he came up with some new guidelines for himself. These were as follows:

1. It is normal to find some people boring sometimes.
2. I do not like everyone I talk to.
3. It is realistic to expect that some people will like me and some people will not.
4. If I continue to talk to people, I will get to know them better.
5. Friendships develop over time, they are not made in a day.
6. I can set the pace at which friendships develop. A little bit at a time suits me best.

Setting Yourself Unrealistic Standards

There are many shy people who feel that they are not "good enough" in some way. Compared to others, they are neither handsome nor beautiful, neither talented nor intelligent, neither rich nor with the right accent. They always manage to be worse off than they believe they ought to be when comparing themselves with others.

Sometimes these shy people have done well at school and were quite popular when younger. However, growing up, they find themselves to be "small fish in a big sea", no longer the brightest, prettiest, or the strongest person around. Rather than realising that it is a common experience for most people to find themselves amongst others who are more intelligent or perhaps more beautiful, they begin to feel inferior and start to downgrade their own good qualities. Or they are people who have always been overshadowed by brothers or sisters who were more talented or attractive than them. As children they were always trying to live up to the expectations of their parents and were given the impression that their achievements were good but not quite good enough for unconditional praise. As adults, they continue to think that there is always another hurdle to be leapt over if they are to be fully acceptable to other people.

40

Many people like this describe themselves as "insecure" or as "loners". The key problem here is not how they behave outwardly but that their attitude towards themselves is unhelpful.

Telling yourself that you always fall short of some arbitrary standard *you* have set will always lower your confidence and make you feel worse about yourself. It may be quite true that you are not the most talented/attractive/intelligent person around but that in itself is not a good reason to be unhappy or to consider yourself less worthwhile. Many thousands of people are happy being average. The opposite is also true; many talented, beautiful people who have all the trappings of success are desperately unhappy and lonely. Having a wonderful job, outstanding intelligence or good looks is not the answer to feeling happy and full of self-confidence. One question that is often asked of people who are lonely, shy and who think they are "not good enough" is "What would you look for in a friend?" No one has ever answered "Good looks, very clever and an expensive car!" Instead the majority answer "Someone who is kind, considerate and who does not take things too seriously."

Put simply, it may be that you consider yourself less acceptable than other people might. You are placing yourself in a very vulnerable and precarious position if your self esteem depends on what other people think of you or if it depends on you always having to be "on top". Setting yourself realistic standards is important. Anyone can get much pleasure out of a sense of having achieved something. Value your strengths and talents, but do not make them all-important.

6. Conversations

For most shy people their biggest problem is talking to others. They often feel apprehensive about meeting people and worry that they will have nothing to say. One fear is that the person to whom they are talking will find them boring and dull. This is often made worse by thinking that, as they do not see many people or do very much, there will not be much to talk about.

The following are some typical thoughts that shy people have; "How do I start?", "I won't have anything to say", "I will sound foolish", "I won't be able to finish", "I will get trapped", "I bet there will be a long uncomfortable silence". All of these worries are bad enough when considering talking to one person, but a whole group of people can be seen as even more daunting. This chapter will provide a simple, easy-to-follow guide to conversations and give advice on how to go about learning to feel more comfortable while talking to other people.

The First Step

The two most important principles when learning any new skill are practising and taking small steps, starting with easy situations and gradually working your way up to difficult ones. With learning to have a conversation it makes sense to start with a very brief conversation and work up from there. There are three basic parts in learning to have a conversation – how to start, what to say, and how to finish. All three are important but it is often the last one, how to finish, that stops may people from even thinking about starting a conversation. It is a common fear that once started, a conversation will get out of control and will grind to a sticky, embarrassing halt with both people wishing they had never started. Such an experience is likely to lead to avoding similar situations for fear of a repeat performance.

How to Stop Once You have Started

Let us first look at ways to finish talking to someone. The aim in ending a conversation is to leave the other person feeling that she or he has enjoyed talking to you and that you also enjoyed yourself. We all know how to say "good-bye", but that is not really enough; you cannot simply say "good-bye" in the middle of a sentence. The thing that matters most is timing, recognising when a break in the conversation has occurred and using it to say a simple concluding remark. Examples of what people say are: "It has been nice talking to you, but I must go now", "I must go now, but I'll talk to you again" or "Well good-bye for now, I'll see you later". A simple "bye" is also possible, but the timing must be right and more importantly, you must make sure your body language is giving the other person the message that you are about to leave. It is important not to give a conflicting message between what you are saying with your body and what you are saying out loud. If you say "good-bye", but stay standing looking at the other person, they will be confused and will not realise that you have finished talking to them. You need to start moving back and maybe turning away slightly as you say good-bye and then take your leave.

What other people are doing and saying provides us with important clues as to whether or not they wish to go. If they are becoming restless and beginning to turn away, then they would probably like to stop talking to you. It is important to remember that the person you are talking to may be as nervous as you and that for him or her finishing off is difficult too. In fact, it is because many of us find this difficult that so many conversations seem to end in an unsatisfactory way. If the person you are talking to becomes restless you should use this as a cue to wind up what you are saying and make a move to go. There are no hard and fast rules; the most important thing to do is pay attention to the situation and to let what is happening dictate your next move.

Starting a Conversation

How do you start a conversation? The most usual way is to use an opening greeting such as "Hi" or "Hello", followed by an opening remark such as "It's nice weather" or by a question like "The bus is taking a long time to come, isn't it?". Questions you could ask obviously depend on the situation. For shy people getting the first few words out can be particularly difficult. Many shy people say things like "I go over and over in my head what I am going to say, yet when I eventually do say it my throat is dry and the words rush out in a croaked jumble." This is a clear example of spending too much time thinking about what to say in an attempt to get it perfect first time. The usual result of this is that the person tries so hard and becomes so anxious that they are bound to make a mess of it. To try and prevent this happening you need to set about practising a few opening lines so that you learn to start a conversation without needing to give much thought to what you say.

For example, imagine meeting someone, a neighbour or colleague at work, and speak to them in your mind. Think about what they might say in reply to you and construct an imaginary conversation in your head. The next step on from this is to start greeting people you meet as part of your daily routine. It can be useful to choose people who you usually see for two reasons: firstly they are familiar to you, secondly, if they are working in a shop for example, they are not likely to be able to stand and talk for a long time. This means that you can practise one aspect of your new conversational skills at a time.

What do I say next? It is in the early stages of a conversation, particularily with someone that you do not know very well, that people have great difficulty in knowing what to say. Shy people often say "I am no good at small talk," or "I never know what to say." To get over this problem there is a need to stop worrying so much about what you should and should not say. "Small talk" is nothing special. It can be seen as a method of "breaking the ice", allowing people who have only recently met to start to learn something about each other.

Many people have a number of stock phrases and themes that they use in the early stages of a conversation with people they do not know very well. Having a readily available supply of things to say allows them to feel more comfortable in social situations. This is because they do not need to worry about having nothing to say. They have a number of things that they are used to saying and have a good idea of the usual responses. This makes it easier to have a smooth-flowing conversation.

It therefore makes sense to build up a variety of phrases and topics that you feel comfortable using to help you to deal more easily with this part of the conversation. If you have no idea what to say, you could go out and find out what other people say. Why not do a little research project over the next few days to discover what sort of things other people say. Listen in when people nearby are talking, at the bus stop, or in a shop. By doing this you will soon get a good range of phrases that people use when they initiate a conversation. Some common ones are; "Lovely weather we are having", "How are you?", with the answer "I'm fine thank you. How are you?", "It is always busy here". Talking about the weather is very common and is always a good topic to start on.

Something else people do early in a conversation is to pay the person they have met a compliment. You could compliment them on what they are wearing, for example saying "I like your shoes." Ideally this should be followed by a question such as "Where did you get them?" which allows the other person an easy reply. If there is food or drink available in the social setting then offering the person you are talking to a drink or a snack can also help to break the ice.

Remember – in the early stages of a conversation it is particularly important to give the person you are talking to the necessary feedback; that is, that you are enjoying talking to him or her, and that you wish to continue. As we have mentioned before, this is done by making sure you look at the person you are talking to and nod and smile appropriately.

Listening

As well as talking there is another equally important aspect of conversational skill; that is, listening. It is important that the other person knows that you are listening to what they are saying and that you are interested. If it is a stranger you are talking to it is worth remembering that he or she may well be as nervous as you are. Looking at the person who is talking to you and nodding and smiling in appropriate places reinforces the message that you are paying attention to what is being said.

Listening is a skill that needs to be practised. If you are not sure how to show that you are listening, look around you the next time you are near groups of people talking and watch them. How can you tell which people are listening? What is it that they are doing? Use the knowledge you gain from this to help you the next time you are talking to someone.

Continuing the Conversation

Once the conversation has started and a few remarks have been exchanged, how do you keep it going? The key to continuing a conversation is to pay attention to what the other person is saying and not pay too much attention to what you will say next. By listening to what the other person says you will quickly learn information that will help you to continue the conversation. Ask them more about things they mention briefly. For example if they were to say "At least this rain is good for my garden", you could ask a question such as "What kind of plants are you putting in for the summer?" Alternatively you could use this as an opportunity for saying something about yourself such as "Yes, my garden really needed some rain." By doing so you are letting the other person know that you have a garden and this establishes something you have in common. This could easily lead to a longer chat about gardens and gardening.

You should try and reply as appropriately as possible. It is confusing to others if you change the topic of conversation abruptly, without warning. Nor should you give a reply to a question that stops the conversation. Many questions can be answered in a variety of ways. Try and avoid using single word answers such as "yes" or "no" as this can have the effect of stopping the conversation. If such a reply is appropriate then make sure you add something else or ask another question as part of your reply. For example if you were asked; "Do you live near here?" your answer might be "Yes, just around the corner. Do you?" Similarly, any questions you ask should not be ones that only need one word answers, unless you intend to follow on with another that allows the person to tell you more.

The suggestions above are only meant as guidelines, they are not supposed to leave you thinking so much about what you will say next that you become anxious. They are things to keep in mind in the early stages of learning to improve your conversational skills. If you have had a bad experience recently while talking to someone it could be worthwhile thinking over what was said, keeping the above points in mind and seeing if you can work out what you might have done better. Put this information to good use by making a mental note of what not to do next time. Remember, mistakes are there to be learnt from.

"Help I'm Stuck!"

Occasionally conversations do become a bit sticky and an awkward silence can develop, making you feel very un- comfortable. Shy people especially hate silences and they tend to assume that they are responsible. Thoughts such as "I'm hopeless at this" or "They will think I am so boring and stupid" run quickly through their minds. *Do not despair,* silences in conversations are very common, especially if two people do not know each other well and you may be much more bothered by the silence than the other person. If you feel you need to break the silence there are a number of ways that you can do this. Reverting back to another stock phrase can be enough to get things going again. Alternatively you can look around you and use what you see to give you a clue as to what to say next. For instance you could comment on a passer-by, or what the person you are talking to is wearing. One way of practising this is to start looking around more when you are out. Learn to notice what goes on around you. Finally, it is always possible that there is nothing more to say. If this is the case why not just finish off the conversation? As you leave the person make sure you remind yourself that you had a nice time talking to someone and that you may well not be as hopeless at conversations as you thought you were.

Introductions

Frequently in social settings the need arises to introduce someone or to be introduced. Many people find this difficult to do. When being introduced to strangers it is a good idea to look at them and smile in acknowledgement. Shaking hands is quite common and is a good way to show that you are friendly. Paying attention to the person's name is also important, so if possible try to use it as soon as you can to help you remember it. Saying something like; "Well John, how long have you lived here?" helps you associate the new name with the new face.

If you are introducing someone make sure you announce both names clearly (this also helps remind you of names). It is possible that you will have forgotten one of the names of the people you are introducing. This is very common and you should not be ashamed of saying something like, "I'm sorry I have forgotten your name". No one will mind this as they too will have had the same experence. A friend of mine often says "I'm sorry I have forgotten your name" and if the person replies John, my friend will say "No, your surname". Or if the reply is the surname he will say "No, I meant your first name."

When you introduce someone it can help things along if you say something about the people you are introducing such as; "This is James, he works beside me. James, this is Bob, he is a plumber."

A Final Word

Everyone is nervous in some social situations, whether it is having to meet your fiance's parents, giving a speech of thanks or meeting someone famous. For most of us the presence of a video camera or tape recorder is enough to reduce us to mumbling, clumsy wrecks. Until, that is, we get used to it with a little practice. The difference between someone who chats happily to anyone and someone who is so anxious they can hardly say a word, is merely a combination of practice and the self-confidence that it brings.

Practice is vital when someone is trying to improve their conversational skills. Most shy people, due to the nature of their problem, do not talk to many people. This means that most social situations, even everyday ones, can be seen as quite threatening. This can result in you feeling anxious, with thoughts that you might make a fool of yourself. This anxiety can easily lead to doing less well than you would have liked to have done. Without a good deal of determination it can mean that you will tend to avoid more social situations and it can soon become a vicious circle. There is a need to make sure that you say to yourself something like, "Well that did not go as well as I would have liked, I must need more practice". Beware of negative thoughts such as "There, I knew I was hopeless at talking to people".

7. Making Friends

We all need friends; people to talk to, confide in, or simply to spend time with. Being lonely and having no friends can quickly lead to feeling isolated and depressed. All of us at some time in our lives feel lonely. Even people who have a wide circle of acquaintances may find that they do not have someone to turn to when they have a problem. One often hears people saying "It's difficult to make friends at my age. Everyone at work goes home to their husbands or families in the evening" or, "I really couldn't tell anyone what was worrying me. They might not be interested and I shouldn't burden them with my problems".

This chapter will look at how you can get to know people better and some of the common problems associated with making friends. It will explore how friendships are made and where you might meet people. Common fears associated with making friends are not knowing where to start, what to say, sounding boring and being afraid that people will not like you. The prospect of making friends can appear such a daunting one that it seems easier to stay indoors and not even try. We hope that by reading this chapter you will gain enough confidence to go out and take the first step towards making friends.

Where to Meet People

Often lonely people who would like to have friends overlook the contacts and acquaintances they already have. Opportunities for making friends arise from the contact we have with other people. Friendships are frequently based on work relationships, or shared interests such as hobbies, and having children at the same school: others are based on living in the same neighbourhood or through family connections. Opportunities can also arise from being introduced to someone through a mutual acquaintance or friend.

To become friends with smeone rather than just an acquaintance requires certain changes in the relationship. With a friend we do not have to behave with any formality, we can just be ourselves without fears of rejection or making fools of ourselves. We do not have to stick to certain topics of conversation such as work or "safe" topics such as television programmes or where we will be going on holiday. Instead, with friends, we can talk about personal topics and reveal more about ourselves. Most people would probably regard their relationships with friends as being special. Friends can often predict what each other will find amusing and what would upset the other person because their knowledge is greater than that of an acquaintance. An acquaintance would only know us in a limited sense and would not have the depth and breadth of knowledge that a friend would have.

It is possible that there are some potential friends among the people and acquaintances with whom you already come into contact in your daily life. One place to start may be with the people who are already around you. However, you may want to meet new people or you may be in a situation where you do not know anyone.

There is a large variety of organisations, many of them national, part of whose function is helping people to meet each other. These range from commercial dating agencies to voluntary organisations for specific categories of people. There is also an enormous range of clubs and societies that meet on a regular basis. It is extremely likely that they would welcome a new face. Look in the local paper and public library for information, choose one that seems interesting and give it a try!

Sometimes clubs hold open evenings to attract new members; watch out for these especially if the idea of just going along is too daunting for you. If you go on one of these nights you can be fairly sure that someone will talk to you and that there will be others there who do not know the ropes yet.

Another way of meeting people is to join a charity or other voluntary group. By their nature, such groups are only too keen to have new members. Again there is something to talk about, and often there are jobs to be done which immediately help to

get you involved and cope with the initial anxiety. A spin-off of such work can be that you end up meeting a large number of strangers by taking part in fund-raising events such as coffee mornings or sponsored walks.

A useful hint is to choose an activity group. Why not try a rambling club or cookery class? It is often easier to chat to someone while you are both doing something. To begin with there is plenty going on around you that you can talk about. Secondly, since there is not a constant pressure to converse all the time, you can put your mind to the task in hand when you need a rest.

Do not be put off by the idea that you will have to make conversation for hours. It is not necessary to talk much the first time that you attend a club or society. The most important thing is to go! You need to see what it is like before you decide if you like it and the people that go there. The first time you go all you need to do is appear friendly and interested. If people do come and talk to you you can ask them more about the club and what it does. The next time you go, if you didn't have too bad a time the first time, you can start talking a little bit more to people that you recognise.

Most local authorities hold evening classes on a wide range of subjects. These are also good places to meet people. Once again they do not require a great deal of social confidence as there is a structured activity. The most important thing is to go a number of times. You will gradually get to know a few faces and when you have the courage you could ask someone to go for a drink or a coffee with you when the class finishes.

Getting to Know People Better

An important place to start in the process of making friends is learning to appear friendly. Often, without realising it, we are giving people the message that we do not want to be spoken to.

How people see us and what kind of person they think we are depends on a number of factors. The initial impression that we give is particularly important. This is mainly determined by our body language (which is explained in Chapter 2). Different postures and facial expressions give different messages to other people. Someone who is standing turned away from you, looking at the floor with shoulders hunched up does not give the message of being friendly. It is unlikely that you would want to approach that person to start a conversation.

Another important aspect of body language is facial expression. It is not too difficult to smile, even if you do not particularly feel like it. Smiling can have a dramatic effect on how a person sees you. By smiling at someone you give the impression to others that you wish to be friendly.

One step on from smiling at people is to say something! It is this part that is hardest for most people who find social situations difficult. Quite often the fear of not knowing what to say is enough to make us avoid the situation completely and stay at home. The chapter on conversations will give you ideas and suggestions as to how to start. Common thoughts that stop people from trying to talk to others are; "What will I say?", "They will think I am boring", "I'm no good at small talk", "What if I start and dry up?". We will now examine worries like these.

The first thing to make clear is that there is no one right thing to say; it is not possible to simply give a list of what to say and when to say it. The right thing to say depends on who you are talking to, where you are, how well you know the people and how they react to what you are saying. Some possible openers might be "I'm new here, have you been here before/for a long time?" or "I don't think we've met before, I'm Jim", or "This place seems quite busy, is it always like this?"

Choosing an appropriate time to approach someone is important. If the person appears busy or in a hurry he or she may not wish to be interrupted nor have the time to chat. Certain situations do lend themselves to chatting more than others, such as coffee breaks or meeting someone in the street on a nice day. If you are unsure of when to approach someone you can always start by asking if it is convenient to talk or if you can join them for a cup of coffee.

It is useful to think of a number of things that you could say to people. A tip here is to use the situation you are in to give you clues about what might be an appropriate thing to say. At first the topics of conversation may still be largely concerned with more concrete, everyday matters such as holidays, the weather, cinema or television, rather than more intimate ones.

The most important thing to do is to take an interest in what the other person is saying. Try to remember what you have been talking about following the conversation. Make a mental note to ask the person something about what they have told you on the next occasion you meet them. Not only will this give the impression that you have taken an interest in them but also it gives you a topic to begin the next conversation with.

More personal information is likely to be exchanged as we get to know people better. Indeed it is unlikely that we would be regarded as a friend by others if more personal information was not exchanged.

Personal information often tells the person how you really feel, think and behave. It goes beyond what we think people may want you to say and may even be contrary to the image that you usually wish to present. On the whole, talking about yourself to someone tends to indicate that you are willing to reveal something of yourself to them and that you expect them to be interested in you. It involves trusting the person to regard what you have said as being private and not for general distribution as gossip. If you do not wish people to know too much about you, then don't tell them too much. You do have a choice in the matter. However, by disclosing things about yourself, you may learn that others also share many of your feelings, thoughts and attitudes.

Choosing who and when to tell is a difficult matter if you would like to make friends. It would not be appropriate to tell your life story or your innermost feelings in great detail to people you had just met. The chances are they would feel overwhelmed, embarrassed and most certainly get the impression that you were more interested in yourself than them.

Take things slowly, step by step. As people tell you about themselves, you can tell them about yourself. You certainly don't need to disclose everything, but only what you want to. You can make the first move in telling someone about yourself. If the person you are talking to then tells you about himself, the chances are that he may be interested in getting to know you as a friend. But if he does not, don't overwhelm him by continuing to talk about yourself. It is always possible to change the topic to a more general one and then take your leave having remained friendly.

An important part of getting to know others is finding out what they enjoy. One good way of consolidating a friendship is doing things that you both enjoy. For example, if you like going to see films, you can ask them if they enjoy that too. If they do, then you can ask them more directly if they would like to come with you to the cinema on a specific day. Of course they may say they don't want to and this could be for a number of reasons such as having a prior arrangement or just because they don't particularly feel like going. This does not necessarily mean they don't like you – it could just mean that they don't want to go to the cinema this time. You can always keep the option open by saying "Another time then".

It is best to try and make the effort to go out if you are asked. It is all too easy to refuse an invitation and stay in and watch television. If you do this more than a couple of times it has three likely effects. Firstly, people are less likely to ask you out again if you have refused in the past as they will assume that you will not go. Secondly, each time you refuse it makes the prospect of accepting the next time even harder. Thirdly, staying in when you wish you had gone out will more than likely leave you feeling quite miserable. If you give in to the feelings of anxiety you have about going out, staying in does not make you feel better. However, what you are doing is reinforcing the idea that going out is not a good thing to do and that staying in is safer. The short term gain of lessening your anxiety does not outweigh the longer term consequences of social isolation and loneliness.

Keeping Friends

It is obviously important to keep in touch with the friends that you have made. This need not be on a daily basis as everyone has other things to do. In general the more frequent the contact between friends, the more likely it is that the relationship will become stronger.

One effect of increasing contact and familiarity with friends is that you will find things that you disagree about as well as agree on. If you can either agree to disagree or if one of you changes his/her opinion then the relationship is likely to become more rewarding. Having similar values and beliefs to those of your friends keeps the relationship going because each person gets support for his viewpoint and feels understood. However, too much agreement and similarity between friends can become boring after a while and a little variety in outlook and attitudes adds interest and is more likely to keep the relationship flourishing.

Friendships will keep going if the relationship continues to be rewarding with both people deriving pleasure from it.

Useful Addresses

A list of some useful organisations is given along with the main contact addresses at the end of the book. It is worth writing and asking for the address of your nearest group. This list is not exhaustive. More information can be obtained from the public library or local newspaper. The Citizens Advice Bureaux also have a lot of information; why not call in or telephone to see what they have to offer? You will find them helpful and full of ideas about what there is to do in your area.

8. Assertion

Few people can say that they behave in an assertive, self-confident manner in all situations. If you are shy, standing up for yourself can be a major problem as it involves putting yourself forward and letting others know what you feel and think. There is a difference between doing this aggressively and doing this assertively. Often people worry that if they speak up for themselves they will be too aggressive and will upset other people. Behaving assertively involves taking other people's feelings into account and not riding rough shod over them.

General Situations

It is easier to stand up for yourself with people you do not know. If a stranger ignores or refuses your request or puts you down it really does not matter a great deal and you can leave the situation without having lost face. They do not know you and so there is no reason to take personally their behaviour towards you. Since it is easier to behave assertively in a situation where you do not know people, this can be a good place to start trying to behave more confidently.

Returning faulty goods

Let us take the example of returning a faulty purchase such as an aerosol to a shop. First of all before you go to the shop it is important to be clear in your own mind exactly what you would like to happen. Do you want a replacement or your money back? Whichever you choose make sure you get that message across. It is probably better not to be over-polite or apologetic as it is not your mistake that the goods are faulty and you may run the risk of having your request ignored or turned down. You might simply say to the assistant "I bought this aerosol last week and it isn't working properly. I would like it replaced please."

Don't be put off by not being sure of what to say. It is often *how* you say something that is just as important. Stand upright and look directly at the person to whom you are speaking. Try not to fidget or shuffle around. Keep your voice steady and clear. One useful strategy you can use if your first request is not granted or you get a blank stare from the assistant is to repeat your request. This has been described as the broken-down record technique! Unless the assistant is particularly awkward, you should get what you want.

It would be a good idea to practise asking for things in shops. A way of doing this would be to deliberately buy something a size too big in a clothes shop and return the next day to change it. Choose a large store that allows people to exchange goods. Remember to keep the receipt to show the assistant when you return the article. This should make you realise that asking for what you want and getting it is not impossible.

Asserting Yourself with People You Know

Behaving in an assertive manner with people you do know involves taking into account the type of relationship that exists between you. Many shy people find it difficult to ask a favour of someone or to say "no" to a request. They often believe that they have no right to make demands on others and yet find it difficult to refuse the demands others make on them. These beliefs may initially seem rather strange and contradictory and yet understanding them is the key to the problem.

Many people who have difficulty asserting themselves describe how saying "no" would make them feel guilty. They believe this would be letting other people down and would mean that they were not "nice" people. Often behind these beliefs there is an assumption that it is their responsibility to please others and that if they do not live up to others' expectations, something awful will happen.

Asking for a favour is just as difficult for many people because it involves asking for special treatment and this carries the risk of being turned down and being left feeling miserable. Also people may think that they have misjudged a relationship if their favour is refused, with considerable embarrassment on both sides. Although these kinds of risks are realistic when asking for a large favour, many unassertive people make the mistake of thinking that the risks are the same when asking for small favours. You do run a small risk whenever you ask a favour. The person could always say "no". If that person were a friend you might well feel hurt and embarrassed particularly if the favour was a small one. In general however, friends tend to be pleased to do small favours. People feel good about themselves when they get an opportunity to do a favour. Let us look at some examples of situations that people find awkward.

Smoking

Take the situation of inviting home someone you know who is a heavy smoker. You know that he will smoke and that you would feel resentful if you were to just grin and bear it. Whatever you do depends on how strongly you feel about smoking. If you know that you will find it necessary to have the curtains dry cleaned afterwards, it is probably better to say something such as "Would you mind not smoking?"

On the other hand you could agree that it is unreasonable to expect someone addicted to cigarettes not to smoke for several hours. You could always try to arrange a compromise and ask them to sit on the other side of the room or not to smoke during a meal.

We have heard of a wedding reception held in a private house at which guests who wished to smoke were directed into the garden! There are many positive ways of dealing with such a situation and whichever you choose depends on how strongly you object. Even such an extreme approach, if done tactfully, is not likely to offend the people in question.

Noisy neighbours

This is an awkward problem. The occasional loud party next door is all right especially if you are invited. However, persistent loud music or overheard domestic arguments can be wearing and difficult to deal with. If your neighbours make a lot of noise late at night and you cannot sleep you could try the following. Knock at the door and politely but firmly say "I would be pleased if the noise can be turned down as neither I nor my family can get to sleep". If your neighbour is reasonable they will do as you ask without making a fuss.

However, sometimes noisy neighbours are not so reasonable and the problem cannot so easily be resolved. A story which comes to mind is of a couple who called in Environmental Health Officers to measure the noise level of their neighbours. In this case the neighbour was a publican and the house next door a pub. After many visits into the pub to ask that the noise of the music be lowered, numerous letters of complaint and only temporary modification of the sound level, they moved house. So even though this couple behaved assertively and did all they could do to change the situation, the problem could not be resolved.

Telephone calls

Most people keep in touch with their family and friends by using the telephone. Some of the best times to catch people at home are mealtimes or in the early evening when the children are being put to bed or before people go out. It is probably fair to add that rather than speaking on the telephone at these times, most people would rather like to be relaxing and enjoying their meal, or are busy with their family. However, rather than making this plain to whoever is telephoning, children are often left in the bath and dinners grow cold because you think that the caller would be offended if you said it was not convenient to speak to them as that time.

One easy solution to this problem is to say politely, "Can I phone you back once I have finished my dinner/put the children to bed?" Given that you have offered to phone back most relatives and friends would not be offended and would agree. Remember, they will also be aware of how difficult it can be when the phone rings and they are busy. If they continue to talk try repeating the message and maybe adding "I really cannot talk just now, I'll ring you in a hour."

To some extent we do have to make allowances for relatives if we want relationships to go smoothly. However this does not mean that we have to put up with being taken advantage of, or them being rude. Letting them know what we like about them is being as assertive as telling them what we dislike. Doing both helps to keep a balance and emphasises that, like ourselves, they are neither all good nor all bad.

Asserting Yourself with Close Friends and Family

One of the benefits of an intimate relationship is that you can often say what you think and feel without risking rejection, ridicule or upsetting the foundation stone of the relationship. There are, however, some relationships in which neither partner expresses either positive or negative feelings towards the other, where anger and resentment build up and are never expressed and where the relationship deteriorates. As a result, people sometimes say "There are no arguments at home", "I could never tell my husband how I feel" or "I have no idea what my wife thinks or feels". Equally often both men and women say that their spouse *should* know how they feel even if they have never said a word to them. This is unrealistic as people cannot read other people's minds, no matter how close the relationship may be.

Learning to express negative and positive feelings in a relationship where these have never or seldom been heard can be difficult. If the relationship has been strained for a length of time and where there is a willingness to make positive changes it may be worthwhile seeking outside help from a marriage guidance counsellor or other professional helper.

Expressing anger

It is healthy to express anger and similar emotions. There are people who never seem to show any signs of anger and who deny that they ever become angry. Controlling or suppressing anger to this extent is unhealthy and often people who behave in this way develop physical problems such as headaches or suffer from stress-related problems such as anxiety.

It is normal to feel angry and if expressed in a direct and honest way, it can be constructive in a relationship. Shouting a torrent of abuse or using physical violence towards someone is *not* constructive and only serves to increase problems between people. An individual who is the recipient of such abuse will either react in an equally violent fashion, which only increases and prolongs the outburst, or will become frightened, resentful and hostile towards the attacker. Either way, the relationship suffers.

If you are angry with someone, it is important to express this directly by saying what it is you are feeling. This helps the other person to understand what it is you are feeling rather than having to guess. It is also vital to make sure you say what you are angry about. If you want to be constructive, be specific about what the person has said or done to make you feel angry.

Telling someone, "I think you are a horrible person" is not constructive as they cannot do anything about that. However, telling someone "I am really angry about you not turning up last night" is constructive as this is a bit of their behaviour that they can change in the future.

Next time you are angry, try expressing it directly by beginnning with one of these statements;

"I feel angry when you do . . ."
"I was really annoyed at . . ."
"I think you have no right to say/do . . ."
"I'm furious with you saying/doing . . ."
"I'm really offended by your saying/doing . . ."

Remember to be specific about what the person has done or said to make you feel angry.

Sometimes it is difficult to express anger immediately. Often we are afraid of not being able to control our angry feelings and imagine that we will lose control. It can be helpful to vent such strong emotion in a physical way. Banging a fist on a table, slamming a door or punching a pillow can help to release this kind of inner tension.

Ideally, anger should be expressed before it reaches a peak, when it becomes more difficult to be specific and constructive. It is always better to express anger spontaneously and directly.

If you have been angry with someone for some time and have never told them how you feel and why you are angry with them, it is certainly not too late to express it. Often a bad situation will only continue unless you do this, as the other person will have little idea of how you are feeling, or have felt. People in this kind of situation often find it difficult to bring up the subject, make excuses that it is too late to mention their anger or that it is no longer relevant. A forthright way to deal with this is to approach the person and express how you have felt. Starting with "I have been wanting to tell you how angry I felt when . . . " may be helpful.

There may be occasions when you have expressed your anger directly and constructively but the other person has responded to this in a mocking or sarcastic manner. This response is often a "put down" and suggests that the other person has difficulty coping with criticism. It also illustrates how even though you can behave in an assertive manner, other people may have difficulties in this area too.

There are several strategies that may be helpful if you are confronted with a sarcastic response. One way of coping is to continue to stand your ground and emphasise how important the issue is to you, for example saying "I can see you are not taking me seriously but I am very angry about . . ." and repeating what you originally said.

Another approach is to comment on the sarcastic response itself and how it makes you feel. A statement like "I am angry with you for trying to put me down in this way but I really want you to know I am serious and want to tell you about what made me feel so angry with you". Alternatively, you could say "I am sorry that

65

you are not taking me seriously, I am wondering whether you find it difficult to discuss this with me," This approach puts the ball back in the other person's court. You can also choose to discuss the issue at another stage. If you do this, it may be better to say why you are postponing raising the issue so that you can leave the situation feeling that you are still in control and not "put down" by the other person. For example saying "I don't want to discuss this with you right now. I'll talk to you another time when we are both ready to discuss it", might be a positive way of leaving the situation.

Receiving criticism

The way in which we respond to someone who is angry with us can also affect the outcome of a confrontation. If someone criticises us and we respond by getting very angry and abusive, the situation is likely to become more heated as tempers rise and may result in physical violence.

We do have the right to defend ourselves and how we do this is critical in bringing about a constructive solution. If the criticism is justified, it is better to acknowledge this immediately rather than try to avoid facing it. This will have the effect of defusing the other person's anger and from there, the problem can be discussed openly and honestly. Simply saying something like "I can see that you are angry about me doing that," lets the other person know that you are taking them seriously and are likely to consider doing something about the problem. If the criticism is unjustified, then you need to be assertive in saying this. If you deny that you did something and the other person believes you are distorting the truth, then an argument will quickly develop where each person defends their position more and more. Again the situation can quickly get out of hand. One tactic to use when criticised unjustly is to be very direct and ask, "Tell me what you think happened?" or "I do not accept your version of this but tell me exactly what you think I did that has made you angry."

By asking for information in this way, you can find out what it is you have done to offend the other person. If they have misinterpreted your actions then you must say so firmly. It can be

helpful to point out that if you had done what they thought you had done, then you could have understood their anger but that this was not what actually happened. So saying "I can see now why you feel angry but I did not do that. The way I see it the situation was like this . . ."

There are occasions when someone is so angry that they may not stop shouting and making accusations in order to listen to what you may have to say. You are unable to defend yourself unless you can be heard. Shouting yourself will only create a more heated situation. One way of getting heard is to hold your hand up and say loudly "Stop" or "Wait". This gives you a chance of breaking into the barrage of complaints. If this does not work, you have every right to get up and go.

Giving and receiving compliments

Many people feel embarrassed about giving a compliment or expressing affection. As these expressions are all too often rare in relationships it is important to be assertive and allow ourselves to express them. If given genuinely and spontaneously, they mean a great deal to other people, helping them to understand how much they are valued and appreciated.

If you are not assertive, you may find this difficult. Often you will have positive feelings towards someone or notice something you like about them but not say anything to them. You may even think that they do not need to know how you feel about them or that they must know by your behaviour towards them that you value them. Everyone needs to know that they are liked and valued, just as you do. Rather than just thinking positive things about someone, act out these thoughts and say something. It does not matter what words you actually use, just say what you are thinking, even if you simply say "You are great.".

People are quite often surprised at being told something about themselves or being complimented. They may even try to dismiss or qualify the compliment by saying "It's nothing really" or "I'm not really like that, it is just a good day I am having." This type of response detracts from what the other person has said and implies they are mistaken. If someone does this when you have paid them a compliment it is often because they do not feel good about themselves, or have had very little positive feedback from other people in the past, and therefore do not know how to respond. Regardless of how you are feeling about yourself, try to be positive in accepting a compliment. Smile at the other person and tell them you appreciate what they have said. You could say "I don't feel very great so it is really nice of you to say that" or "That is nice to hear". Be assertive in accepting compliments. The person giving you positive feedback in the form of a compliment is telling you how they value you or what they like about you and the least you can do is accept their praise. They have a right to give their opinion and no one is suggesting you will become conceited if you believe them.

9. Dating

If talking to people in general is a problem when you are shy, then asking someone for a date is really difficult. You will be much more likely to be anxious if you are talking to someone who you would like to go out with. Most people experience great difficulty asking someone they like out because they place so much importance on the outcome.

Where can I find someone? In the chapter on making friends a number of suggestions are made on how to go about meeting new people. The advice in this chapter applies equally well to the problem of finding a suitable partner. On the assumption that you prefer the company of people with similar interests, the best places are those where people with similar interests to yourself are likely to be. If you do not go out socially at the moment, it is definitely worth considering joining a club or going to evening classes or some similar activity. There are a number of more specialised agencies whose function is to provide people with the chance to meet prospective partners. Computer dating agencies are used by many people and may be worth considering. Most dating agencies accept that you may not like the first person that you arrange to meet and will provide a choice of people whom they believe you might get on well with. You are under no obligation to date, or even to arrange to meet, any of the people the agency suggests. However, using an agency might provide you with an opportunity to meet some new people. Attending a club or going to an evening class can be equally good or perhaps an even better way of meeting people because the circumstances are more natural. There is not the same pressure to like and get on with the other person, and the relationship has time to develop.

Asking Somebody Out

How do you ask someone out? Where do you go? When do you ask them? What if they say no? What if they say yes? These are all questions that go through a shy person's mind when they meet someone they want to ask out. There are no hard and fast rules as to what to say. However, there are some basic things to keep in mind. It is worth remembering that asking someone out for the first time is bound to be difficult. If you know any couples, you could ask them what happend when they first went out. This will help you see that they too were nervous about asking someone out and being asked out. It might also give you some idea as to what you could do on your first date.

What do I say? The best thing is to be specific. Decide what you would like to do or where you would like to go, taking into account what the other person might like, such as going for a coffee or going to the cinema. Approach the person then and ask them if they would like to go with you. If possible, this should be when they are on their own. You should have a clear idea of *where* you want to go and *when*. This is better than saying "Would you like to come out with me sometime?" This is because a vague question like this could be answered with a "yes" but you still have not actually made an arrangement. The activity you choose depends on what you and the person you are asking out would like to do. You should have a fairly good idea of what this might be if you have spent time talking to them before you decide to ask them out. If you are very shy it is a good idea to choose an activity that encourages you to have conversations but also includes something that would see you through the quiet patches. Going to the cinema or theatre is good as most of the evening is spent watching something and at the end of the show there is a readily available topic of conversation to help things along. Ten pin bowling and ice-skating allow a good deal of spontaneous conversation and the chance to do something together.

Do I go on my own or do I go with a crowd?

It is not really a good idea to go with a large crowd if you are shy, even more so if the other person is also quiet. It might be difficult for you to get any time to talk and to get to know them better. Secondly, if your interest is having a more serious relationship with them, by asking them out on their own you are giving a clear message that it is only their company that you are really interested in. On the other hand if you are in a crowd of people, you need not do all the talking and this can take the pressure off you. Nevertheless, you do need to make sure that you spend some time talking to the person you have asked out or they will feel ignored.

What if they say yes?

It might sound odd, but if the person you are asking out does agree to accompany you, you might suddenly be lost for words. To avoid this happening it is best to have clear in your mind what the specific arrangements will be. This includes deciding where you will meet the person or whether you will pick them up from their house. You also need to decide the time, allowing for buses and so on. If you are meeting them in town choose a place that has shelter in case the weather is bad. Remember that most people do not like going into pubs on their own. Having thought this all through it is a lot easier when the person says "yes" to reply by making a clear arrangement, stating time and place.

What if they say no?

There are a number of reasons why a person might say no if you ask them out. It does not always mean that they do not like you. It may be that they have other arrangements, that they are feeling tired or that they do not have enough money to go out. However, they may have said no because they do not want to go out with you. If this is the case do not despair, look upon your request as practice and use it to good effect for the next person you decide to ask out. If the time you have chosen is not convenient then you should ask them what time would be better and arrange to go out when it suits both of you. Or if they cannot manage to go out with you because of other reasons such as a lack of money try to suggest an alternative, bearing this in mind.

Being Asked Out

Being asked out on a date by someone can be just as big a problem as asking somebody out. First of all you need to decide whether you like the person enough to go out with them. If the answer is yes, then your reply should of course be "Yes, I would like that" or something similar, remembering to look pleased as you reply.

How do I say no?

It is refusing to go out with someone that can be particularly difficult for shy people. You need to be clear in your mind why you don't want to go. If it is because the time or place is not suitable, then you should say so and suggest an alternative. However, if you are not interested in going out with the person you must make this quite clear. It is a common worry at this point that the other person's feelings will be hurt if they are turned down. There is no doubt that the correct thing to do in this situation is to do what *you* want to do. To do anything other than this will only lead to problems in the future. Yes, it may upset the other person but it is better that they know sooner rather than later that you do not want to go out with them. Many people find that they are unable to say "no", and instead make up an excuse such as "I am busy just now." This is not really a satisfactory way of turning someone down as it is not clear whether you are saying that it is not convenient or that you do not want to go out with them at all. It is far better to pluck up courage and state simply that you would *not* like to go out with them. It is polite to thank them for asking you, but probably adds to the confusion to start a long rambling explanation as to why this is the case. You might like to say a little about why you do not want to go, such as "It is nice of you to ask but I am not really interested in going out with anyone at the moment". Chapter 8, on assertion, looks at the problems of saying no in a more general sense.

Do they like me?

Does the person that you have asked out like you? It is always hard to tell whether the person you are out with actually likes you and by how much. There are two ways to answer this question, the first is simply to ask the person whether they like you or not. This is not appropriate on your first date, but if you have been out a number of times it would be. The second way to answer this question is to look at the evidence. If they have agreed to go out with you a number of times and are also asking you out then it is highly likely that they like you. If they are enjoying themselves and seem keen to go out again, then they must like you.

How much do they like me?

This is a much harder question to answer, and you will only find this out over time. If going out together becomes a regular thing and you start making plans for the future together, then it is very probable they like you a lot. The only sure way that someone knows that the person they are going out with likes them a lot is when they say so. If things are going well it would be appropriate to tell the other person how you feel about them and how much you enjoy their company. If they respond to this with enthusiasm and tell you how much they like you, things really are going well.

What will I say?

The main thing to bear in mind when going out with someone in the hope of building up a relationship is to show the person that you are interested in them. Do not spend a long time before you go out worrying what you will say. If you get on well you will be less anxious and find that your conversation flows easily. Remember, if you are stuck there will be plenty going on around you which you can talk about. You do not need to talk all the time, sitting quietly together can be enjoyable. Think about what they have told you about themselves and try to ask them questions that follow a similar theme. It is not a good idea to ask very personal questions too soon. Take your time, if all goes well you will be seeing the person on a number of occasions, and there will be plenty of time to talk about more personal matters. On the first two or three dates conversation should be kept to general topics. If you are worrying about what you will say, remind yourself that there are two people involved in a conversation and that you will not need to do all the talking. Indeed, if you were to do so it would not create a very good impression.

Don't Go Too Fast

A mistake shy people sometimes make is trying to go too fast in a relationship. Sometimes they spend such a long time plucking up the courage to ask somebody out, that when the person they have chosen says yes, they assume that they are in love with them. This is unlikely to be the case; love at first sight is rare. Most relationships develop gradually as two people get to know each other better. If someone has agreed to go out with you then you should look upon this as a starting point and try not to get too carried away with the idea that before long you will be walking down the aisle. The other person has to decide whether they like you and you need to get to know them better to decide how you really feel and whether it is them as a person you like or simply the idea of a relationship. The usual course of events is to go out with someone a number of times before you both feel that you know each other well. Most relationships seem to take on a life of their own and either become more serious or fade away through time. If you do know any couples it might be worth asking them at what point they knew things were going well. Most couples are unable to tell you the precise time they knew the other person liked them enough for the relationship to develop into a more serious one.

Being Honest

In all relationships it is important to be as honest as you can. This is for two main reasons, firstly, because the other person needs to know how you feel and think, and secondly, if you are honest it encourages your partner to be honest with you. If in the early stages of going out with somebody there are things you like about them, then why not tell them? Should there be anything that you are not happy with, then say so as soon as possible. Similarly, if it becomes apparent that the person feels more seriously about you than you feel about them, tell them so.

Being honest with yourself is equally important. You may be able to convince yourself in the short term that you are having a good time, but if this is not the case, you will eventually become very dissatisfied with the relationship. If the person you are going out with tells you that he or she only wants friendship from the relationship, then agree to it only if you honestly know that is all you want. It is not a good idea to pretend to be happy with a casual relationship when you would really like the relationship to be more serious.

Increasing Intimacy

As you get to know someone better, you may want to increase intimacy through touch. Some of the problems that can arise, and ideas for coping, were dealt with in Chapter 2.

Sex

When you are going out with somebody on a regular basis the issue of sex may crop up. It can occur sooner than you expect. Honesty in sexual relationships is important. If both people are happy to embark on a sexual relationship there are no real problems. It is important to discuss the method of birth control to avoid unwanted pregnancy as a result of mistaken assumptions. However, a problem may arise if one of the partners does not want the relationship to develop into a sexual one when the other partner does. This can occur very early on in dating. It is important to be honest with yourself and your partner at this point and to state your feelings clearly. If you do not feel ready to embark on a sexual relationship you must say so. It may be helpful to give your reasons for refusing and make it clear if you think that you may be willing to do so in the future. It might be helpful to say to your partner, "If you loved me, you wouldn't try to persuade me to have sex with you just now". If your partner provides you with the ultimatum of either having a sexual relationship or ending the relationship altogether, you may not want to continue having a relationship with a person who does not take your feelings into account.

Sometimes a problem arises when you feel that you should be in a sexual relationship although it has not yet been mentioned. There is not a certain stage in a relationship where sex is vital. Some people go out with each other for many years without having a sexual relationship. Although it is not as common as it used to be, some people wait until they are married before they have sex. If you are having particular problems with the sexual side of your relationship we suggest you read something on the subject, such as the book in this series "Coping with Sexual Relationships" by Dr Judy Greenwood.

Ending a Relationship

All relationships between two people either become long term or finish. It is likely that you will have a number of relationships which end before you have a long term relationship which may lead to marriage. This is not always the case. Some people settle into a long term relationship with the first person they go out with, but it is more common to have several relationships before finally settling down. You learn from every relationship and over time each one helps you mature and become more confident. You will also mature over a period of time and you may find that the person you would like to have a long term relationship with in your twenties may be very different from the one you wanted in your teens.

Ending a relationship or being told that a relationship is over can be difficult to cope with. If the person you have been going out with tells you that they no longer want to spend time with you, then it is best to accept what they say. Usually they will have thought it through and will have decided what they want. It is often not wise to spend a long time trying to persuade them to change their mind. If you suspect that they do not really want to finish with you, one possibility is to suggest that you both think about things and arrange a time to meet and discuss it further. This is appropriate when there has been an argument and decisions have been made in the heat of the moment.

Telling somebody that you no longer wish to go out with them is difficult and no matter how you do it you are likely to be very worried about hurting the other person's feelings. As with refusing to go out with someone, it is best to let the other person know how you feel as soon as possible. It is certainly better for you, but it is also better for them as it is wrong for them to think that you want to go out with them when this is not the case. It is best to come straight to the point when you are ending a relationship and not try to explain all the reasons as this can leave you fumbling for words and may mean that you do not say what you want to. It is of course only fair to let the other person know your reasons. You should try to state clearly and briefly your reasons for wishing to end the relationship without getting involved in long explanations.

10. Self Help

Introduction

Throughout this book the emphasis has been on ways you can go about helping yourself to overcome particular problems you may have. The best way to learn a new skill is to avoid tackling too many problems at once. Setting realistic goals and taking things slowly, one step at a time, will be the most helpful strategy to adopt. In this way you will be able to tackle the more difficult problems with increasing confidence. Going too fast is likely to increase the number of problems that you have and you may be put off trying to change. In the past you may have tried to help yourself but failed. A common reason for failure is not that people cannot change by helping themselves, but that they have been trying to tackle too many problems too soon.

Often it is easier to go about changing how we behave if we can clearly identify the specific problems we wish to work on and the steps that will lead us to cope with them in a better way. This chapter consists of a number of practical tasks to allow you to do this. Read through the whole chapter before you decide which sections would be of most help to you. You can either write directly in the book or make copies of the forms you wish to use and carry them around with you.

Basic Techniques

In general, it is a good idea to use a pen and paper to note what your problems are in order to get your thoughts clear. The simple act of writing things down allows you to see more clearly what is wrong. This helps you to stand back and look at your problems as if they were someone else's. In order to be good at helping yourself you need to learn to look at your problems in the most unbiased way possible. That is to say, you need to find the facts of the situation without letting your lack of confidence, anxiety or low mood influence you too much. Some people find that after writing down the facts about what is bothering them, they begin to realise that the problem is not as big as it seemed.

Make a List

Lists are extremely useful in any self-help programme. When you decide to sit down and work out what your problems are, make a few lists. Firstly, list everything that you find difficult, in simple language. Secondly, list things that you would like to be able to do. Thirdly, list things that you can already do, in other words, your good points and strengths. A way of making the first list is to take a blank sheet of paper and write; "I find it difficult to . . ." a number of times down one side. Then you just finish the sentences with whatever comes into your head when you read the first part. For the list of things you would like to be able to do you could start with "I would like to . . .". For the third list you could use a sentence beginning with; "I can . . .", or "I like doing . . ." An example of the first type of list, the problem list is given in Figure 1.

- I find it difficult to . . . *speak to strangers.*

- I find it difficult to . . . *say no to my boss.*

- I find it difficult to . . . *order food in a restaurant.*

- I find it difficult to . . . *return faulty things to a shop.*

- I find it difficult to . . . *talk to women I find attractive.*

- I find it difficult to . . . *be in a very crowded room.*

- I find it difficult to . . .

- I find it difficult to . . .

- I find it difficult to . . .

- I find it difficult to . . .

Fig. 1

It is possible to use the first list to help you draw up the second list if you are finding this difficult. To do this, rewrite the problems from the first list into things you would like to do. For example changing "I find it difficult to talk to women I find attractive" into "I would like to be able to talk to women I find attractive without stammering." Having a list of what you would like to achieve is the first step in planning your self-help programme. Once you have done this you are in a good position to work towards finding a solution.

Try it yourself and see how you get on. Before you start the list you may think that everything is wrong, but there are probably only a limited number of problems to work on. Make sure you also make a list of what you can do and what you enjoy doing to remind yourself of your good points.

There are other lists that you could make to help yourself. What about a list of things to talk about when you first meet someone, or a list of places that you would like to visit or things you would like to do, but have never got round to doing? You could also draw up a list of people you know.

Keep a Diary

A diary can be used to help you in two ways. Firstly, it can be used to write down how you feel each day and to help you get your thoughts clear. Secondly, a diary can be used as a way of keeping track of your progress. If you are shy and lonely then there may not be anyone close to you who can tell you how well you are doing. If you are keeping a written record you can use it to look back and see how far you have progressed. This is especially helpful for those days when you feel really hopeless and think you have achieved nothing. A quick read through your diary will be sure to show you that you have come further than you think.

A tip when keeping a diary is to write down one positive thing that has happened each day to help you learn to think more positively and to increase your self-confidence. For example, you might write down "I spoke to my neighbour today" or "Did well at work" or "Someone said I looked nice" and so on. No matter how bad a day it has seemed to be, there is bound to be something positive, even if it is only that you got out of bed before tea-time!

An example of a possible diary page is given below.

Date *2nd August*

Today I felt quite miserable when I woke up because it was the weekend and I had nothing planned.

After getting up, I decided I needed to do something positive.

I wrote down a list of things I needed to do and then chose one with a pin!! . . . It was mending my bicycle!! I also decided that I would speak to my neighbour if I saw him. (The thought of this made me feel quite nervous).

(later on) . . . What a good day! I mended my bicycle and when my neighbour passed he said "Good morning," and I managed to reply. Then we started chatting. It was difficult at first, but it turned out that he is a keen cyclist and we talked easily about cycling. The best thing is that we have arranged to go for a cycle run tomorrow!!

Positive things. I mended my bicycle *and* spoke to my neighbour *and* have something to do tomorrow.

A Step-by-Step Programme

In all self-help plans it is important to take things slowly, step by step. To help you do this it is useful to arrange the list of things that you find difficult in order of difficulty, with the least hard things first, progressing gradually to the most difficult. This allows you to see more clearly what the small steps will be and stops you trying to do something too difficult too soon. To help you make this list you could use the form in Figure 2. In Figure 3 there is an example of a completed form. Notice how each step is slightly harder than the one before, eventually getting to the target chosen in Part 2 of the form.

PART 1. What do you find difficult to do?

PART 2. More specifically, what would you like to be able to do by the end of your programme (your target)?

PART 3. Now think of something that is to do with what you have written in Part 1, but that would only be a little difficult to do.

1. Write it here ....

Now think of something that would be slightly harder than what you have written for number 1.

2. Write it here ....

Continue down the page writing down slightly harder things each time until you get to the target you put down in Part 2.

3. ....

4. ....

5. ....

6. ....

7. ....

8. ....

9. ....

10. ....

Fig. 2

An Example of the Step-by-Step Programme

PART 1.   What do you find difficult to do?
Speaking to women I find attractive without stammering.

PART 2.   More specifically, what would you like to be able to do by the end of your programme (your target)?
Say something nice to Sarah without stammering.

PART 3.   Now think of something that is to do with what you have written in Part 1, but that would only be a little difficult to do.
1. Write it here; *Speak to Julie in the office. (She is attractive, but I do not fancy her.)*

Now think of something that would be slightly harder than what you have written for number 1.
2. Write it here; *Go to Julie's office when her friend Sarah (whom I fancy) is there.*

Continue down the page writing down slightly harder things each time until you get to the target you put down for Part 2.
3. *Talk to Julie and Sarah in J's office.*
4. *Next time I see Sarah in the corridor, say hello and smile.*
5. *Say hello, smile and say to Sarah "Off to see Julie?" when I next pass her in the corridor.*
6. *Pay Sarah a compliment the next time she is in Julie's office.*

Fig. 3

Setting targets

Once you have your plan of action the next problem is keeping to it! To help you do this you can keep a record of *when* you hope to do each step of your plan. Remember that social interactions cannot be totally planned in advance as it depends on what other people are doing. You may have to make opportunities as well as take them as they arise. You can also use this form to record when you have done each step to show you what progress you are making. Using your answers on the form in Figure 2, and your list of things you would like to achieve, decide what your targets will be. That is to say, what you hope to do and by when. This should be in the same order as in your step-by-step programme. You should allow yourself a column to note if the opportunity never arose. Write this down on a sheet of paper like the example in Figure 4.

The targets you choose should be clear, precise ones. For example, rather than decide your target will be " go to a class", be more definite and say something like "go to the community centre on Monday and enrol for the pottery class." Another example might be making your target "Arrange with John to go out on Sunday, when I see him on Friday morning" rather than the more vague "Ask John out." This way you will be more likely to do what you have decided as you will have it clear in your mind exactly what you expect to achieve. This allows you to prepare yourself by thinking the task through. The only thing left to do is to get on with it! Making sure you put a tick against each thing you do.

Target	Date to be done by	Done	Not Possible
Speak to neighbour	Monday		X
Write about Club	Wednesday	X	
Speak to newsagent	Friday		
Go out with Jim to coffee shop on Saturday at 11 a.m.	Saturday		

Fig. 4

Using the step-by-step approach and setting target dates and times can be used to help you overcome a variety of different problems. What is good about these methods is that they are designed by you so they suit you. You could use them to help you with anxiety problems, difficulties with different people, places and so on.

Solving problems

Sometimes we are faced with a problem for which we cannot clearly see the answer. You may have a few ideas, but which one is the best? Where do you start? There is a pen and paper technique that can be used to help you see what the best solution to your problem might be. It works as follows;

STEP 1.   Write down clearly what the problem is.

STEP 2.   Make a list of as many possible solutions as you can think of, include anything that comes to mind, no matter how silly they seem to be. Use what you have learnt by reading this book to help you.

STEP 3.   Once you have made the list go back and read through each idea and practise in your mind what might happen if you used the idea. Give each one a rating out of 10, the higher the number the better the solution.

STEP 4.   Now decide to try out the solution with the highest mark out of 10.

STEP 5.   Once you have tried the solution you chose go back and make a note of the outcome. If it worked, well done! If not, then try and work out what went wrong, and by using what you have leart pick another solution and give it a try. This might have to be repeated a number of times before you make it.

Think positively!

Some people, especially those who are feeling anxious, depressed or lacking in self-confidence, have a tendency to view things very negatively. They can have negative thoughts about their abilities that can have the effect of slowing their progress down or making them feel so hopeless that they do not bother trying. Examples of such thoughts are "I'm hopeless, I'll never get over being shy", "I'm still anxious, I'm a real mess", "It is all my own fault I'm like this, no one else feels this way". These thoughts tend to pass through our minds very quickly and often without us being aware of thinking them. If we listen to and believe such thoughts we very likely end up feeling more hopeless and depressed. This is mainly due to our tendency to believe the worst about ourselves when we are feeling low.

The first step in trying to deal with these negative thoughts is to learn to recognise when they occur. The next time you feel particularly hopeless try to think about what was going through your mind. You may well discover you had been thinking very negatively. Not everyone can immediately become aware of these negative thoughts, it usually takes a little practice to work out what it was you were actually thinking that has led you to feel how you do in a particular situation.

In the chapter on social anxiety we mention thoughts that increase the anxiety someone might feel in a social situation. An example might be thinking "I'll make a fool of myself if I speak up". This is another type of negative thought and can be dealt with in the same way.

A third type of negative thinking is to always believe the worst possible explanation when something happens. An example of this might be passing someone you know in the street and not being greeted by them. If your self-confidence is low you may automatically think "He doesn't like me, no one likes me". However there may be other explanations as to why you were not greeted, such as: they may be short-sighted and even though they were looking straight at you they could not see you. It could be that they were deep in thought or that as you were not in your work clothes they did not recognise you. There are a number of possible explanations, not all of them meaning you are hopeless and that the person does not like you.

The following technique will help you see that there are other ways of looking at things instead of always believing the first negative thought you have. It involves thinking of other, more rational answers to the first thought you had. Asking yourself what evidence there is for what you thought is a good start. To help you along you can use a simple two column system like the example given in Figure 5.

First Thought	Sensible Answer
I'll never get better.	*I have a good chance of improving if I try to help myself consistently.*
There is no point in trying.	*If I don't try, how will I know if I can improve?*
No one likes me.	*I don't know many people so how do I know if this is true? John called on me last week so he probably likes me.*
I have nothing interesting to say.	*It might seem that way to me, but it is probably just because I feel so low that I think this.*

Fig. 5

Coping with the bad days

During your self-help programme things will not go smoothly all the time. You will have the occasional day when things go badly. This will happen more frequently when you first start helping yourself. The main reason for people failing when they are helping themselves is the effect minor setbacks have on them. There is a tendency to give up completely if something goes wrong.

To prevent this happening realise from the start that there will be bad days. Get it clear in your mind that your progress will vary and that sometimes things might go wrong. If you can do this then you will not be completely taken aback when they do go wrong.

When things go badly, there are a couple of things you should do. Firstly, remind yourself that it is not day to day progress that matters but how you are doing overall. Think of what you have managed to do that you could not do before you started. Also, tell yourself that you had expected some bad days so the fact that you have had one should not be so surprising. Secondly, use your bad experience as a way of learning more about yourself and your problems. Go back over what went wrong in a constructive way and see what you could do next time to improve matters. By doing this you will be turning a "bad" day into a useful experience that will help you in the future. Finally, remember one bad day or even a bad week does not mean that the next day will not be a good one.

11. Further Help

You should have read most of this book by now and be beginning to put some of the suggestions made into practice. For most people this book will be enough to help them help themselves. It is of course important to remember that change does not happen overnight. Instead step-by-step practice, persistence and patience are likely to be rewarded by increasing self-confidence and more satisfying relationships.

There will also be some people who will require more specialist help to overcome their shyness or loneliness. It may be a good idea to explain the problem to your general practitioner. Certainly doctors are now very aware that this kind of problem can lead to poor mental and physical health. For example, sometimes people who feel lonely may also suffer from depression. Amongst other symptoms, they may experience a low mood, feel sad and hopeless, have lost their interest in life and blame themselves for the way things are. They may also find it difficult to motivate themselves to do anything about these problems and think that very little can be done, so there is no point in trying. A doctor would be able to disentangle whether the problem of loneliness was being aggravated by depression and if it was, he could offer to treat the depression. Once a person is less depressed she or he will be more able to mix with other people and once again have the choice of developing satisfying friendships.

Your doctor will most certainly have had other patients come for help with their shyness, social anxiety and loneliness. Many doctors now refer people who suffer from these problems to clinical psychologists. Clinical psychologists have degrees in psychology and further clinical training which combines scientific methods with clinical practice. They offer specialist help to people who suffer from social phobias, anxiety and shyness. Sometimes this is done individually and sometimes in groups with other people who have the same problem. The idea of helping people who are anxious with others who suffer from shyness in a group may seem very threatening; however the benefits are quickly realised. In a group you can meet other people who suffer from the same problem and this can help to reduce the feeling that many people have of being all alone in the world with their problem. More importantly, a group setting helps people to test out their newly acquired social skills in a "safe" therapeutic environment without fear of rejection or harsh criticism. Everyone is encouraged to try things and to give feedback on how to improve their skills even further.

If you wish further help, speak to your doctor first. He may refer you to a clinical psychologist for more specialist help such as anxiety management or social skills training, or to another professional who may offer a similar kind of service.

Useful Addresses

Here is a list of organisations which may be helpful for two reasons. Firstly, if you have a problem in a particular area there is likely to be a self-help group or organisation near you. Secondly, many organisations welcome volunteers and this is a good way of making friends.

National Federation of 18+ Groups of Great Britain (for people aged 18 to 30)
Nicholson House
Old Court Road
Newent
Gloucestershire
Tel. 0531 821210 (24 hours)

Age Concern (England) (for the elderly)
60 Pitcairn Road
Mitcham
Surrey
CR4 3LL
Tel. 01-640 5431

Age Concern (Scotland) (for the elderly)
33 Castle Street
Edinburgh
EH2 3DN
Tel. 031 225 5000

Alcoholics Anonymous
P.O. Box 1
Stonebow House
Stonebow
York
YO1 2NJ
Tel. 0904 644026/7/8/9

Cruse (for widows, widowers and their children)
Cruse House
126 Sheen Road
Richmond
TW9 1UR
Tel. 01-940 4818/9047

Gamblers Anonymous
17/23 Blantyre Street
London SW3
Tel. 01-581 3660

Gingerbread (single parents)
35 Wellington Street
London
WC2E 7BN
Tel. 01-240 0953

National Friend (for homosexuals)
BM Friend
London
WC1N 3XX
Tel. 01-359 7371

National Housewives Register
("for lively-minded women")
c/o Antoinette Ferraro
245 Warwick Road
Solihull
West Midlands
B92 7AH
Tel. 021 706 1101

Solo Clubs (divorced, widowed or separated)
Room 8
Ruskin Chambers
191 Corporation Street
Birmingham
B4 6RY
Tel. 021 236 2879

National Association of Widows
Headquarter Office
Voluntary Service Centre
Chell Road
Stafford
ST16 2QA
Tel. 0785 45465

Volunteer Centre
29 Lower Kings Road
Berkhamstead
Herts
HP4 2AB
Tel. 04427 73311

National Council for the Divorced and Separated
13 High Street
Little Shelford
Cambridge
CB2 5ES

British Association of the Hard of Hearing
(B.A.H.O.H.)
16 Park Street
Windsor
Berks
SL4 1LU

Further Reading

SHYNESS AND LONELINESS

On Your Own
(A practical guide to
independent living)

Jean Shapiro
(Pandora Press, 1985)

Meeting People is Fun
(How to overcome shyness)

Dr Phyllis M. Shaw
(Sheldon Press, 1979)

The Shy Person's Guide to Life

Michael Bentine
(Grafton, 1985)

Beginnings
(A book for widows)

B. J. Wylie
(Allen & Unwin, 1986)

Loneliness

Dr Tony Lake
(Sheldon Press, 1980)

BODY LANGUAGE

Teach Yourself Body Language

G. Wainwright
(Hodder & Stoughton, 1985)

Body Language

Julius Fast
(Pan, 1972)

Body Language:
How to read others thoughts
by their gestures

Allan Pease
(Sheldon Press, 1984)

*The Pocket Guide to
Manwatching*

Desmond Morris
(Grafton, 1982)

ASSERTIVENESS
Your Perfect Right
(A guide to assertive
behaviour)

R.E. Alberti & M.L. Emmons
(Impact, 1970)

*Don't Say "Yes" When You Want
To Say "No"*

H. Fensterheim and J. Baer
(Futura, 1975)

How To Stand Up For Yourself

Dr Paul Hauck
(Sheldon Press, 1981)

Assert Yourself

Gail Lindenfield
(Self Help Associates, 1986)

ANXIETY
Self Help For Your Nerves

Dr Claire Weeks
(Angus & Robertson, 1962)

RELATIONSHIPS
Staying Together
(A practical way to make your
relationship stay together)

Reginald Beech
(Wiley, 1985)